JUST LEAD!

JUST LEAD!

A NO-WHINING, NO-COMPLAINING, NO-NONSENSE PRACTICAL GUIDE FOR WOMEN LEADERS IN THE CHURCH

Sherry Surratt and Jenni Catron

Foreword by Mark Batterson

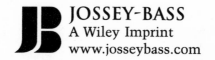

JOSSEY-BASS
A Wiley Imprint
www.josseybass.com

Published by Jossey-Bass
A Wiley Imprint
One Montgomery Street, Suite 1200, San Francisco, CA 94104-4594—www.josseybass.com

Jossey-Bass books and products are available through most bookstores. To contact Jossey-Bass directly call our Customer Care Department within the U.S. at 800-956-7739, outside the U.S. at 317-572-3986, or fax 317-572-4002.

Wiley publishes in a variety of print and electronic formats and by print-on-demand. Some material included with standard print versions of this book may not be included in e-books or in print-on-demand. If this book refers to media such as a CD or DVD that is not included in the version you purchased, you may download this material at http://booksupport.wiley.com. For more information about Wiley products, visit www.wiley.com.

Library of Congress Cataloging-in-Publication Data has been applied for and is on file with the Library of Congress.
ISBN 978-1-118-31439-5 (cloth); 978-1-118-42003-4 (ebk); 978-1-118-42180-2 (ebk); 978-1-118-43391-1 (ebk)

Printed in the United States of America
FIRST EDITION
HB Printing 10 9 8 7 6 5 4 3 2 1

LEADERSHIP NETWORK TITLES

The Blogging Church: Sharing the Story of Your Church Through Blogs, Brian Bailey and Terry Storch

Church Turned Inside Out: A Guide for Designers, Refiners, and Re-Aligners, Linda Bergquist and Allan Karr

Leading from the Second Chair: Serving Your Church, Fulfilling Your Role, and Realizing Your Dreams, Mike Bonem and Roger Patterson

In Pursuit of Great AND Godly Leadership: Tapping the Wisdom of the World for the Kingdom of God, Mike Bonem

Hybrid Church: The Fusion of Intimacy and Impact, Dave Browning

The Way of Jesus: A Journey of Freedom for Pilgrims and Wanderers, Jonathan S. Campbell with Jennifer Campbell

Cracking Your Church's Culture Code: Seven Keys to Unleashing Vision and Inspiration, Samuel R. Chand

Leading the Team-Based Church: How Pastors and Church Staffs Can Grow Together into a Powerful Fellowship of Leaders, George Cladis

Organic Church: Growing Faith Where Life Happens, Neil Cole

Church 3.0: Upgrades for the Future of the Church, Neil Cole

Journeys to Significance: Charting a Leadership Course from the Life of Paul, Neil Cole

Church Transfusion: Changing Your Church Organically—from the Inside Out, Neil Cole and Phil Helfer

Off-Road Disciplines: Spiritual Adventures of Missional Leaders, Earl Creps

Reverse Mentoring: How Young Leaders Can Transform the Church and Why We Should Let Them, Earl Creps

Building a Healthy Multi-Ethnic Church: Mandate, Commitments, and Practices of a Diverse Congregation, Mark DeYmaz

Prodigal Christianity: Ten Signposts into the Missional Frontier, David E. Fitch and Geoffrey Holsclaw

Leading Congregational Change Workbook, James H. Furr, Mike Bonem, and Jim Herrington

The Tangible Kingdom: Creating Incarnational Community, Hugh Halter and Matt Smay

Baby Boomers and Beyond: Tapping the Ministry Talents and Passions of Adults over Fifty, Amy Hanson

Leading Congregational Change: A Practical Guide for the Transformational Journey, Jim Herrington, Mike Bonem, and James H. Furr

The Leader's Journey: Accepting the Call to Personal and Congregational Transformation, Jim Herrington, Robert Creech, and Trisha Taylor

The Permanent Revolution: Apostolic Imagination and Practice for the 21st Century, Alan Hirsch and Tim Catchim

Whole Church: Leading from Fragmentation to Engagement, Mel Lawrenz

Culture Shift: Transforming Your Church from the Inside Out, Robert Lewis and Wayne Cordeiro, with Warren Bird

Church Unique: How Missional Leaders Cast Vision, Capture Culture, and Create Movement, Will Mancini

A New Kind of Christian: A Tale of Two Friends on a Spiritual Journey, Brian D. McLaren

The Story We Find Ourselves In: Further Adventures of a New Kind of Christian, Brian D. McLaren

Missional Communities: The Rise of the Post-Congregational Church, Reggie McNeal

Missional Renaissance: Changing the Scorecard for the Church, Reggie McNeal

Practicing Greatness: 7 Disciplines of Extraordinary Spiritual Leaders, Reggie McNeal

The Present Future: Six Tough Questions for the Church, Reggie McNeal

A Work of Heart: Understanding How God Shapes Spiritual Leaders, Reggie McNeal

The Millennium Matrix: Reclaiming the Past, Reframing the Future of the Church, M. Rex Miller

Your Church in Rhythm: The Forgotten Dimensions of Seasons and Cycles, Bruce B. Miller

Shaped by God's Heart: The Passion and Practices of Missional Churches, Milfred Minatrea

The Missional Leader: Equipping Your Church to Reach a Changing World, Alan J. Roxburgh and Fred Romanuk

Missional Map-Making: Skills for Leading in Times of Transition, Alan J. Roxburgh

Relational Intelligence: How Leaders Can Expand Their Influence Through a New Way of Being Smart, Steve Saccone

The Post-Black and Post-White Church: Becoming the Beloved Community in a Multi-Ethnic World, Efrem Smith

Viral Churches: Helping Church Planters Become Movement Makers, Ed Stetzer and Warren Bird

Just Lead! A No-Whining, No-Complaining, No-Nonsense Practical Guide for Women Leaders in the Church, Sherry Surratt and Jenni Catron

The Externally Focused Quest: Becoming the Best Church for the Community, Eric Swanson and Rick Rusaw

The Ascent of a Leader: How Ordinary Relationships Develop Extraordinary Character and Influence, Bill Thrall, Bruce McNicol, and Ken McElrath

Beyond Megachurch Myths: What We Can Learn from America's Largest Churches, Scott Thumma and Dave Travis

The Other 80 Percent: Turning Your Church's Spectators into Active Participants, Scott Thumma and Warren Bird

Better Together: Making Church Mergers Work, Jim Tomberlin and Warren Bird

The Elephant in the Boardroom: Speaking the Unspoken About Pastoral Transitions, Carolyn Weese and J. Russell Crabtree

CONTENTS

ABOUT THE JOSSEY-BASS LEADERSHIP NETWORK SERIES

Leadership Network's mission is to accelerate the impact of 100X leaders. These high-capacity leaders are like the hundredfold crop that comes from seed planted in good soil as Jesus described in Matthew 13:8.

Leadership Network

- Explores the "what's next?" of what could be
- Creates "aha!" environments for collaborative discovery
- Works with exceptional "positive deviants"
- Invests in the success of others through generous relationships
- Pursues big impact through measurable kingdom results
- Strives to model Jesus through all we do

Believing that meaningful conversations and strategic connections can change the world, we seek to help leaders navigate the future by exploring new ideas and finding application for each unique context. Through collaborative meetings and processes, leaders map future possibilities and challenge one another to action that accelerates fruitfulness and effectiveness. Leadership Network shares the learnings and inspiration with others through our books, concept papers, research reports, e-newsletters, podcasts, videos, and online experiences. This in turn generates a ripple effect of new conversations and further influence.

In 1996, Leadership Network established a partnership with Jossey-Bass, a Wiley Imprint, to develop a series of creative books that would provide thought leadership to innovators in church ministry. *Leadership Network Publications* present *thoroughly researched and innovative concepts* from leading thinkers, practitioners, and pioneering churches.

To learn more about Leadership Network go to www .leadnet.org

FOREWORD

Whenever pastors get together, leadership development is one of the main topics of discussion. We want to know how to develop more and better leaders. The irony is that most churches have a mostly untapped resource of highly capable leaders already sitting in their sanctuary every Sunday morning: women. Regardless of your theology or culture, women can play a major role in leading your church in fulfilling its God-given mission. Many churches struggle in successfully integrating women with strong leadership gifts into an often male-dominated culture. The key question is how men and women can lead together in the context of the local church.

Although we see women in key leadership roles throughout the Bible, the challenges of men and women working together in the context of the local church are real and often complex. That's why I'm excited about this book. I am passionate about seeing leaders, regardless of their gender, grow to their full potential in Christ. I see the difference strong women leaders make every day at National Community Church (NCC), the church I pastor in Washington D.C. We have as many women on staff as we do men. And women have played key leadership roles in all of our small groups and ministries. We wouldn't be who we are or where we are without their leadership. We'd literally be half the church we are today without their leadership!

I also know firsthand how challenging it can be for men and women to work alongside each other in the local church. We need a leadership field guide to help reach our maximum effectiveness for the Kingdom. Sherry Surratt and Jenni Catron are the ideal leaders to write that field guide. Together they have over forty years of experience leading in a variety of roles in the local church, and they connect with women leaders across the country and around the world. NCC has benefited directly from their wisdom and experience. But more than their experience, their attitude set Sherry and Jenni apart. The bottom line for them isn't to win a theological argument over the role of women but to further the Gospel mission of the local church. They are all about seeing people come to faith and grow into mature disciples, and they want to see women equipped to do their part.

My hope is that churches will use this book as a practical guide in engaging men and women leaders to fulfill their God-given Kingdom mission. I have seen the difference effective women leaders make at both NCC and churches across the country. Regardless of your theological or cultural lens, this is a challenge worth taking on.

Mark Batterson
Senior Pastor
National Community Church
Washington D.C.

PREFACE

This book began a few years ago while both of us were attending a multisite conference at Seacoast Church in Charleston, South Carolina. As is usually the case, I (Jenni) was the only woman among the group from my church. When I was told that I really needed to meet Sherry Surratt, I jumped at the chance. I tracked her down after one of the sessions she was teaching. I was eager to meet this incredibly kind and dynamic female leader whom everyone was raving about. She seemed equally as excited to meet me, and we instantly became friends.

Although we live in different parts of the country, we found ways to connect with one another as often as possible. Our conversations inevitably led us to discussing the burden that we shared in helping to encourage and support other women leaders. We each had countless stories of conversations over coffee (Sherry) or tea (Jenni) with hundreds of other women leaders who were trying to find their way in ministry leadership.

Our hearts ached over the loneliness, isolation, and insecurity that seemed to be holding so many women back from truly leading from their gifts and calling. We longed for the comfort and camaraderie of a safe place—a circle of other women leaders who share the same struggles and joys of leadership.

Just Lead! is the conversation we would have with you if we could sit down together over a cup of tea or coffee. There is much we could share: the joys and pains that we have felt as women leaders, the struggles and successes that we've experienced, and the lessons we wished we could have learned through others rather than learning the hard way.

We believe in you—in your gifts, calling, and purpose as a leader. We believe God has placed you where you lead and wants you to thrive there. We hope this book will be a source of strength, encouragement, some laughs, and perhaps a few tears. We subtitled the book *A No-Whining, No-Complaining, No-Nonsense Practical Guide for Women Leaders in the Church* because we want to equip you to get the job done that God has called you to. Don't let the enemy convince you that you are alone, or misunderstood, or insignificant. Although there are certainly moments that feel that way (we've had our share!), it's simply not true. Most important, we hope that this book will be a reminder to you that you are not alone. You have dear friends and champions who love you, are cheering for you, and are praying over you.

We hope that *Just Lead!* will provide you with practical leadership help to develop the skills to lead yourself and others with the character, confidence, and authenticity of a godly woman. Each chapter addresses a different hurdle that we've encountered as women leaders. We'll share personal stories as well as weave in stories from other amazing women leaders. At the end of each chapter are questions for personal reflection and group discussion. Take the time to reflect on and process each challenge and identify situations in your own leadership where you've encountered this issue. Then find another woman leader or gather a small group of women leaders and discuss a chapter each week over lunch. Our prayer is for this book to be a source of encouragement and hope when you find yourself in challenging moments of leadership. We hope that you will be inspired to *just lead!*

ACKNOWLEDGMENTS

Jenni Catron

Anything important in life cannot be accomplished without great people around you. That has never been truer for me than in writing this, my first book:

To my amazing husband, Merlyn: you have sacrificed greatly while always, always cheering me on and celebrating every step of this journey. Thank you for understanding and embracing these dreams with me. I love you!

To my family, who taught me some of my earliest leadership lessons and pushed me to be my best in everything, thank you.

To my baby sister, Jessica (aka Hilda), thank you for being the first person I tried to lead and still loving me anyway.

To the leaders who have poured into my life—teachers, professors, bosses, and mentors: Thank you for seeing in me what I couldn't see.

To my "Golden Girls," Rachel, Sus, and Shelby, who love me the same whether I lead or not, who have watched me grow and been faithful supporters every step of the way. I love you girls dearly!

To my pastor, Pete Wilson, and the amazing team at Cross Point: thank you for your grace in the good and the bad days of my leadership. You guys are the best staff on earth!

To my greatest champions and cheerleaders—Tami Heim, Shannon Litton, Kat Davis, Ashley Warren, and Stephen Brewster: everyone should have someone like you in their life. Thank you for always believing the best.

Sherry Surratt

It is amazing how God places us in the exact right family and circle of friends to provide exactly what we need:

To my amazing husband, Geoff: you are my forever friend and love of my life. Thanks for believing in me even when I didn't.

To my talented son, Mike: you amaze me every day with your brilliance and your dedication to God. I'm proud of you.

To my brilliant daughter, Brittainy, and daughter-in-love, Hilary: you both will change the world with your leadership. Dream big!

To the most amazing granddaughter, Maggie Claire: I hope someday you'll see in yourself what I do: your brilliance, your talent, your potential.

To the women in my life who have inspired and challenged me: Betsy, Lisa, Sibyl, Julianna, Cynthia, Tammy, and so many more. I am grateful to all of you.

From Both of Us

We are blessed to have had many amazing people speak into this project:

To the Leadership Network team—Mark Sweeney, Greg Ligon, and Stephanie Jackson: thank you for spurring us on to this project and believing in the importance of this book.

To Sheryl Fullerton and the Jossey-Bass team: thank you for your constant guidance and encouragement every step of the way. Thank you for capturing the vision of this project.

To the amazing women who allowed us to interview them and were willing to share their stories: thank you. Your stories will inspire thousands more to just lead.

To the women leaders around the world whom we've connected with via the blog, e-mail, a phone call, hallway conversation, or over a cup of tea: your passion is what made this book possible. You have been a gift to us; this is our gift to you.

INTRODUCTION

◆

HUMBLE BEGINNINGS AND BIG LESSONS

The conversations and requests are too numerous to count: the woman who pulls us aside after we speak at a conference or retreat, the young businesswoman from our congregation who asks to meet over coffee, the e-mail requests for mentoring, the constant pleas for a conference—all asking about the development of women leaders. Why, they ask, hasn't more been written on this subject? We've wondered that too, and this is why we've decided to share our story, along with the wisdom and lessons learned from other great women leaders who've crossed our path. Women pastors, business professionals, directors, leaders in their community and churches, women courageous enough to step up and lead. Women like you.

And so we start with a short version of our own stories. Sherry began as a fourth-grade teacher and public school administrator, moved to pastor on staff at a large multisite church, then became a director at Leadership Network, a Christian nonprofit organization that helps church leaders grow and innovate, and connected with hundreds of women leaders across the nation along the way. Jenni began as a young professional in the Nashville recording industry who moved to the executive staff at one of the fastest-growing churches in the Nashville, Tennessee, area, overseeing pastoral and ministry staff and launching their multisite ministry.

We're not fooled by our résumés. We struggle with insecurity and indecision, and we make mistakes just like everyone else. But in the chapters that follow in which we share our stories, we hope that as we laugh at ourselves and candidly share our mistakes and what we've learned, you'll learn with us. We tackle the big stuff in this book: leadership hurdles that threatened to choke us, how we learned to lead ourselves and others (including men), sprinkled with inspiring leadership stories from awesome women leaders who've taught us great lessons. Our hope is that God will somehow use our words to stir your heart and ignite your God-given passion for leading, just as he has done in us. And so we begin.

SHERRY'S STORY

I'll never forget the day my mom came home from a parent conference with my kindergarten teacher. She gently sat me down and said, "We need to talk about your bossiness." It was the beginning of numerous future conversations that went something like this:

"Sherry, you can't tell the teacher she's telling the story wrong."
"It's not your job to teach the first-grade class the correct way to
    say the Pledge of Allegiance."
"Did you really tell the principal you were going to reorganize the
    lunchroom and start a revolution for free pizza on Fridays?"

My poor mom. She was having to corral a daughter who desperately wanted to run the world but had the finesse of a ticked-off rhinoceros in a china closet. I was a budding young pot stirrer who couldn't stand to see opportunities go by or miss the chance to try out a new idea. I often inspired others to jump in with me, like the time I talked my best friend into getting up and dancing in the middle of the church Christmas play, in which we were both playing sheep. This role did not call for dancing, but I thought the play needed jazzing up a bit. During the ensuing scolding that came my way after the play was over, I should have learned some lessons about self-control and obedience, but instead I remember thinking, *Cool. I can talk people into stuff.*

Does this ring any bells? If you're reading this book, you've probably had big ideas yourself and discovered your ability to inspire others to join you. You've probably also noticed other things, such as your ability to seize an opportunity and lead others through indecision and chaos. You may find yourself getting frustrated in situations where the lack of leadership is apparent and get itchy when progress or resolution seems distant. It's okay. You're a leader, and you're in good company.

For me, it started with a small epiphany in seventh-grade world history class. The teacher had just put us in discussion groups, where I think we were supposed to write a one-paragraph solution for world peace (at least that's what I heard him say). He instructed us to arrange our chairs in circles and then choose someone to lead the discussion questions on the worksheet. We arranged. We sat. We fidgeted. I remember thinking, *Should I speak up?* But the words from so long ago—"we need to talk about your bossiness"—rang in my ears, and I hesitated. Finally, the girl who was getting full enjoyment from her gum (the one I referred to as Miss SnapCracklePop) turned to me and said, "You do it. I don't want to." The circle of heads agreed with lethargic nods, except for the boy seated next to me who had already melted into a coma of boredom. And then it hit me: I *wanted* to do it. I loved every opportunity to lead, even if it was corralling a herd of seventh graders in a quest for a ten-sentence solution for a universal peace treaty. I was a leader.

But somewhere along the way, something had sunk into my heart and head. It was this: Be careful. You don't want to be perceived as that bossy girl, the know-it-all, the show-off.

My first leadership lesson came to me when I was nineteen years old from a beautiful, take-charge person of confidence named Jeanette, my youth pastor's wife. She asked me to lead the children's choir and assist in directing the upcoming musical they would perform in the adult service. The kids ranged in age from kindergartners to sixth graders and were noisy, boisterous, and quite vocal in their skepticism that I could lead them in anything, much less a musical production. Jeanette came to my aid after one spectacularly unproductive choir practice when I think I said something like, "Um, would anybody, like to, um, sing?" It was, of course, a question that I never should have asked, and it was met with a resounding NO! She quietly observed the chaos, then gently chided me with some simple words: "You're the leader. So lead."

These words came back to me again and again as I fumbled my way through leadership moments as a classroom teacher and administrator in an inner-city school system. There were those moments of hesitation when I held back because I didn't want to appear too overbearing or bossy. There were also moments of indecision because I lacked experience and was too insecure to ask for help. I knew I was the leader, so why didn't I just lead? I wanted to, but the fact remained that sometimes I just wasn't equipped. While I may have had the ability to lead a wiggly group of unenthusiastic children in a choir song, I was often ill equipped to make a confident decision under pressure or lead a mixed-gender team that didn't know how to work together. Why didn't I ask for help? Because I felt the same way you've probably felt: *I should know how to do this!*

Really? Just because we have the desire, does it also mean we have the skill? I've learned over the past thirty years of leadership that Jeanette's words were laden with responsibility. "So lead" also meant, "So grow" and "So learn," and I needed to do both. More than just developing confidence and gaining experience through time, I needed to learn at the feet of master leaders, both men and women, and humbly allow God to break my pride and shape my character so I could be used by him. I also needed to study the practical skills of leading, knowing when to speak up, and understanding when to lean into the wisdom of others.

I wish I could say this has been a swift, easy journey for me. It hasn't. That sassy, strong-willed, bossy girl followed me into adulthood, even though I didn't invite her. Looking back, I see a picture of pride and arrogance mixed with dollops of insecurity and fear. It wasn't a pretty picture. But my God is an awesome God. He placed incredible leaders in my life and allowed me ringside seats to view their talents.

My first teaching position was under a principal who led in the face of incredible financial and socioeconomic roadblocks but was never too stressed to respond with grace and dignity. My area superintendent taught me that people matter more than process. God placed other brave souls in my path to say in various ways, "We need to talk about your bossiness," as well as a variety of other issues. He has let me walk through mistakes and blunders to see clearly the need for his workmanship in my life. Thank goodness.

God created in me the desire and raw talent to lead, just as he has in you. And just as he provided the small boy with a lunch of bread and fish and the ability to share, he can transform anything inside us into something big enough to meet the need if only we'll offer it. And just as the landowner passed out talents to his servants and expected great returns, God is asking us to do something with what he has given us: not to dig a hole and keep it a secret or pretend with false humility that we aren't able, and not to hide in a corner because we're afraid someone will point a finger and label us bossy. But to use our creativity and ability to learn, grow, and become the leader God designed us to be.

This is not an easy journey. But that's okay. You're up to the challenge, and we're excited you've chosen to join us.

JENNI'S STORY

My story doesn't start out all that different from Sherry's. I too remember the inner turmoil of a strong-willed leader in a little person's body. But unlike Bossy-Pants Sherry (she knows I love her so I can get away with that), I was outwardly Little Miss Goody Two-Shoes—the compliant, obedient child in public who wrestled privately with a sense of responsibility to lead. And that's what it was for me: a responsibility.

My mom used to say to me all the time, "Others may; you cannot." I remember trying to understand the logic behind that statement. What sense does that make? It was equal to a phrase I'm sure you might have heard when you were growing up—the all-familiar "because I said so." I think parents throughout the ages have used that one when they're just flabbergasted enough to try to put an end to a tiresome conversation. If you're a mom, you probably have a phrase like that too. Although in my mind "others may, you cannot" was not a strong argument, I understood that when Mom said it to me, the argument (or lack thereof) was over.

I couldn't shake that annoying little phrase, which communicated a standard to me that I've carried forward into all of life. Perhaps Mom saw the leadership potential in me and was determined to hold me to a high standard. Perhaps it was just her way to get me to move on and drop whatever teenage plea for freedom I was advocating that day, but either way, it became a measuring stick for how I approached life. It was the first indication to me that I was made to be a leader. The Goody Two-Shoes in me couldn't ignore the sense of responsibility I felt to use my influence wisely.

I didn't even know the word *leader* in those early years. Where I was growing up in a small midwestern town, we didn't talk a lot about leaders. Our primarily blue-collar community talked a lot about "the boss man" and the supervisors whom the regular folk seemed to dislike. I didn't hear adults talk about leadership or the influence of it, and I certainly didn't hear them talk with fondness about those in authority.

And yet I remember seeing leadership in others around me. I was drawn to it even though I couldn't explain what it was. It was Bonnie, the owner of the ice cream shop where I worked throughout high school. She had remarkably kind eyes and an even bigger heart. She showered me with opportunities, infused confidence, and saw gifts in me that were otherwise undeveloped. She took risks, and she made tough calls. She believed in her team, and I had no doubt that she believed in me. Bonnie taught me what it meant to lead in a way that left others encouraged and inspired.

There was leadership from my great-uncle Tom, who was also my piano and voice teacher. He was easily in his mid-eighties, and I remember being terrified of finding him dead when I showed up for my after school lesson. (No joke: in the mind of a ten year old, eighty was freakishly old!) But Uncle Tom was a spry old guy who was determined to help me develop my gifts. My fondest memories of him happened to be my worst nightmares back then. He had a way of keeping me on my toes and teaching me to always be prepared. He was most famous for matter-of-factly telling me as I entered church for the Sunday evening service that I would be singing that night. No warning. No preparation. If I was lucky, he would tell me *what* I was singing before I actually got on stage and heard the first note from the piano. Uncle Tom's expectations taught me to be ready, prepared, and confident to be in front of others—to lead.

And then there was Greg, the president of ForeFront Records. I had dreamed of working for this company since I was thirteen years old. I literally had landed my dream job and wasn't remotely equipped to do it, but Greg saw something in me that I didn't see in myself. I'll never forget the first solo business trip that he allowed me to accompany one of our recording artists. In preparation for the trip, he sat me down and explained in great detail the weight of the responsibility I was assuming and the details I needed to attend to; then, with a strong pat on the back, he told me he believed that I would do a great job. I remember every moment of that trip: the plane ride to Chicago during which I thoroughly reviewed our schedule; the drive from the airport to the hotel, terrified I'd total the rental car or end up somewhere in the cornfields of Iowa; greeting the artist at the hotel and driving her in downtown Chicago in search of a specific Chinese restaurant she wanted to eat at; and hosting a day full of meetings that left me exhausted and yet completely satisfied. I could do it! I really could lead. This was a feeling that was new, exciting, and terrifying all at the same time.

Looking back, I see leaders throughout my life, but I wouldn't have known to label them as such. Leaders make life better. They believe and develop. They identify giftedness and call it out. Leaders leave the world and others better as a result of their presence, and they influence those they love.

Sometimes the word *leadership* is scary. That seems to be especially true for women. Maybe it's because of the gross feelings of inadequacy and insecurity we tend to wrestle with. Perhaps it's because society, culture, and the church have been slow to endow us with this title. But for whatever reason, a lot of us run away from it. This makes me angry for you, one of our world's best leaders. It makes me angry for all of us: the world that needs us to come out of the shadows and be the leaders we were created to be.

History is riddled with amazing women leaders who somehow busted through the resistance and barriers they faced. Consider Deborah, a prophet, priest, and judge of Israel who led God's people to forty years of freedom. There was Queen Elizabeth I who boldly defended her faith and saved England from ruin, and

Joan of Arc who at the tender age of seventeen gave up her life for France's freedom. And no one can forget the amazing Mother Teresa who selflessly served and modeled what it means to be the hands and feet of Jesus Christ to a depraved world.

These are only a handful of stories, but stories that reassure us that God designed women to lead. He designed us to use our place of influence to change lives. How would the world be so much less if they hadn't emerged from the shadows to boldly do what they were called to do?

Before you feel completely intimidated by these outstanding examples, unsure that you are called to lead, think of a woman in your life who has made a marked difference for you. What would your life have been like if she hadn't noticed you, affirmed your gifts, challenged your strengths, and kicked you in the pants when you needed it? Perhaps it was a teacher, a coach, an aunt, your mom, a boss, a friend. Whoever she was, she led you to a place you had never been before. She led you to something that you didn't see possible. She inspired hope and infused confidence. That's what leaders do.

And I bet you have it in you too. I don't think you would have picked up this book or someone wouldn't have handed it to you if it wasn't in you somewhere. We hope to take you on a journey that challenges you to lead well wherever you are. Our paths may look different from one another's but you have a sphere of influence, a circle of people who are looking to you and desperate for you to call them to greatness.

When we talk about leaders throughout this book, we are talking about you. Sure, there might be some things that don't specifically apply to your role as a leader, but tuck those nuggets away for the day that they might be helpful. And what about the voices in *your* head? For Sherry, it was the "don't be the bossy girl" voice. For me, it was my mom's voice reminding me I was set apart as a leader. Whether your voices are positive or negative, we know you have them. What will you do with them? Will you let these voices limit you or inspire you to greatness? And the question is no longer, "Are you a leader?" it is whether you're ready to be a great one.

Are you ready for this journey? If so, let's come out of the shadows and just lead!

QUESTIONS FOR REFLECTION AND DISCUSSION

1. Are there voices that have influenced your feelings about your leadership? Have they come from others or from you?
2. Do you remember a moment early in your life when you knew you were a leader? What feelings did it evoke then?
3. Who have been the early influencers in your leadership development? Have you taken the time to thank them?

CHAPTER
1

ONLY THE LONELY

For the first time, I (Sherry) walked into the room that was to be my office for the next school year. It was big and empty and smelled like paper and glue. I remember hearing a soft echo as I plunked my purse and briefcase on my desk, and thought to myself, *This is perfect. A nice quiet space to organize, concentrate, and get stuff done.* And so it began.

This was my first year as assistant principal at the urban elementary school where I had been teaching for five years, and I was ready to change the world in my new role. As I began to organize and unpack the few boxes I had brought with me, my principal walked in. After her greeting, she let me know that we'd meet for our first official administrative team meeting in fifteen minutes. I was one of two assistant administrators for this large school with one thousand students, and I was looking forward to working with my counterpart, an older, more experienced administrator. As I prepared to join my principal for the meeting, I noticed stacks of files being brought in and wondered briefly what they were for.

The meeting remains a blur in my mind. I jotted notes furiously as assignments came my way: sort the files, design new processes, meet with the upper-level team leaders, be ready to communicate my new discipline strategy (I remember wishing I had one). The list seemed endless. So many terms and titles were thrown my way, and out of the corner of my eye, I glanced at Geri, the other assistant principal, sitting calm, cool, and collected with high-heeled shoes perfectly matching her smart outfit. I decided to follow her lead. Take detailed notes. Give a slight nod of the head indicating complete understanding. Don't ask any questions. Respond with "of course" when my principal asked if I understood. But I didn't. I was lost.

FEELING ALONE

The first day of school came with the excitement of new books, sharpened pencils, and shiny lunchboxes. I was looking forward to connecting with my former team of fourth-grade teachers, but when their lunch break came, I was in a parent conference. The first week brought an all-staff planning meeting after school, and after I gave assignments and everyone split into their grade-level teams, I had a strange thought: now that I lead the teams, I don't belong on one. I hovered over the circles and occasionally joined a discussion, but I felt like the odd woman out.

Have you ever felt like this as a leader? Perhaps it's a vague sense of isolation because your role has changed and removed you from the familiarity of your former team. Or you are not quite comfortable in the role of leading others older and more experienced than you. Maybe the isolation is partly due to the facade you feel you have to keep in place that says, "I know what I'm doing. I have it all under control."

LEAD ALONE OR LEAD WELL

I experienced my first dose of intense isolation at the first district meeting of administrators. With dozens of schools spread around the Houston, Texas, area, our gathering numbered about sixty. Right away I noticed a couple of things. I was one of the youngest in the room, and though this was a profession typically comprising females, I was one of the few at the administrative level. I wondered briefly if I was dressed appropriately and all of sudden wished I looked older. As I looked around the room, it seemed from the chit-chat that everyone else already knew each other, so I found a seat and sank into it. I immediately dropped my purse. Not only was the noise loud, but the amount of stuff that rolled out was mind-boggling: five ballpoint pens, two of them broken; an empty tape dispenser; and a pair of sunglasses with one lens missing.

The discussion started, and I instinctively reached for one of the pens. I took copious notes, trying to track the threads of discussion and unfamiliar academic terms. This was my habit: don't ask about things you didn't understand, but research them later so no one will know you didn't know them. The discussion swirled around the room, with many of the men interrupting each other and stating their opinions firmly. It was easy to see their passion and love for their individual schools, and they didn't hesitate to disagree or offer an idea they thought was better. But I didn't say a word. I sat quietly observing, feeling younger and greener than I had ever before felt in my life.

I had landed this position because I had caught the attention of my district superintendent, an astute leader who didn't really care about traditional methodology and was constantly on the lookout for fresh ideas and a new approach. His sprawling inner-city district was struggling with test scores, but his concern went deeper than that. He had a passion for students to develop a deep love for reading and experience the true joy of learning. Two years before, I had devised some strategies to help struggling students with reading comprehension and was able to share them with not only my class but my grade level and eventually the entire school. I took the boring rules of comprehension strategy and put them into rhymes and games that engaged the students' imagination, and slowly we saw our test scores climb and students take pride in their reading accomplishments. This visionary leader had taken note that I could see through the old ways and dream about the new. He saw leadership in me and called it out.

But this day, he was not impressed. He had been in the meeting and even directed a question my way about reading strategies, giving me an open door to speak up. But I was sure my ideas were small and would expose my lack of experience in a room full of brilliant men and women with years of teaching under their belts. Surely they had implemented far better ideas than I had ever thought of. I was young, I was new, and I figured I was better off staying quiet.

He didn't say anything after the meeting and waited a few weeks before coming into my office. He asked how I was doing and how I felt about my new position. The truth was I felt lonely. I missed the camaraderie of being part of my fourth-grade teaching team. I felt isolated in the overwhelming pressure of having to figure things out for myself. I felt paralyzed when confronted with complex situations and daily fought the urge to ask somebody else (somebody older and wiser) to make the decisions for me. I'm sure I didn't communicate very well what my struggles were, but I think he already knew them anyway. He began to ask some pointed questions. Who was I connecting with to ask for help? Had I done any research to find other young administrators like myself to talk to? Who were my leadership mentors? I had to admit I had reached out to no one. He then said some words that I thought about for a long time afterward: "Sherry, you can lead alone, or you can lead well."

Those were some big words to chew on. If what he said was true, and I've come to believe they are, I was limiting my own performance. I was making assumptions that my gender and age were debilitating factors and allowing myself to become an island. I was overwhelmed and not reaching out for help. I was trying to figure it out alone, forgetting that everyone starts somewhere, and if I were to look around, I'd see that I was surrounded by dozens of brilliant leaders who could help me.

Though that conversation was hard, I let it be a beginning for me. I began to reach out and ask questions. I connected with other young leaders within my district and formed professional relationships with leaders in other organizations who could help me. I found a mentor who loved the Lord with all her heart and freely shared her wisdom. I also took a hard look at myself. I had to admit it was pride that made me think I had to have all the answers and give the appearance that I always had everything under control. It was way past time to give that up to God.

A STORY OF LEADING WELL

I'm forever intrigued by sharp women leaders who don't fall into the traps I did, especially those who make bold moves and lean into the wisdom of others without hesitation. One such leader is Linda Rankin, a young, petite blonde from San Diego, California, who serves as the campus development director at Eastlake Church.

Linda's Story

The first time Linda and I met, I loved her confident smile that accompanied her quick wit and the fact that she cracked a joke within our first few minutes of conversation. As she shared her leadership journey with me, I was struck by how open she was to the leadership lessons that came her way.

❖

I first joined the church staff at Eastlake after serving as a family ministry volunteer for several years. My background was education, and I was quite happy as a teacher to upper elementary students, so when the offer came to join Eastlake, I hesitated. I knew I was being called into ministry, but was this the right opportunity? I wouldn't have called myself a leader at the time, but in the Christian school where I taught, the other teachers looked up to me and often sought me out for advice and counsel and to be their spokesperson to the principal. God was definitely doing work in my heart. As I was finishing the school year, I got a call from my executive pastor, who asked me to come and help manage the family ministry staff while they looked for their next family ministry pastor. I wasn't sure I was up to this, but I felt God calling me.

In this position, I served as the mediator between the executive pastor and the family ministry staff. I sat in on interviews and asked questions, learning much about managing people and handling conflict. We quickly found our next family pastor, but shortly after the transition, I was again approached by the executive pastor, who said, "Linda, you are already leading our family ministry. Why don't we just hire you?" We rearranged our new hire to lead in another area, and I was moved into the family ministry position. I knew I was getting incredible opportunities because I was being faithful and following where God was leading me.

I wish I could say everything went smoothly from here on, but it didn't. My husband and I were struggling in our marriage and not sure where to turn. But again God provided. I was now part of a staff that was caring and supportive. Even through our family difficulties and my obvious distraction, I was trusted, developed, and saw my leadership responsibilities increase. I leaned into this support and shared my struggles openly, knowing that this was a risk. Sometimes in leadership, you can get sidelined if you are dealing with personal issues, but this wasn't the case here. My senior pastor and executive team gave me wise counsel, allowing me to develop at my own pace, giving me encouragement and support every step of the way. I'm thankful God helped me to be open and share my struggles.

The opportunity came to go with my executive pastor who felt called to step in as senior pastor of a church in the Seattle, Washington, area. I agreed to go with him for a year as his executive director as he worked on helping this traditional church make a transition to a more contemporary model. We felt this would be a great opportunity as a family for a fresh start, and so, holding tight to God's hand, we made the move. Did I feel qualified? No. Was I willing to work hard and learn quickly? Absolutely.

Our time line was quick. I had to learn new things in a very short amount of time. I had to, as Mike Bonem says in *Leading from the Second Chair*, "grow deep but also go wide," becoming an expert in some areas while retaining a visionary aerial view over many.[1] I feel that I grew the most during this time. I was working long hours and learning new things every day. By making this move of obedience, God helped me grow in knowledge and also gave our family time to heal and grow together. I will always look back on this experience as a learning lab time in my leadership. It was a bold, scary move for our family, but God works miracles when we're not afraid to step out in faith!

After our first year of a successful launch and transition, we decided to move back to San Diego. I had learned much about developing systems and leaders and implementing strategy and was invited to join the executive team at Eastlake. Looking back to my teaching years, I wouldn't have labeled myself a leader, but I was now comfortable with the title. God had done amazing work in me. I would now be the only woman on this team, but I wasn't fearful about this and had confidence that I was a leader with bold ideas who could execute them well.

People have asked me how I handle being the only woman on an all-male executive team. Staying true to who God made me to be, I look and act like a woman, but there are times when I've learned to control my emotions to match those of the men in the room. There's a fine balance of getting your point across but not elevating the emotion, always communicating that your goal is to help. I'm one of the youngest members on this team, but instead of letting my age or gender isolate me, I lean into them as assets. My team listens when I try to bring a next-generation female's view to the discussion, and I know this view brings value to the discussions. I try always to communicate my respect and earn my seat at the table with a high level of integrity.

I sometimes struggle with the loneliness of leadership and turn to God often. There's heaviness with the confidentiality that comes with sensitive information. There are also disagreements. At the end of the day, if I've disagreed with the way a decision has gone, I feel lonely. We want our opinion to matter. When we feel strongly and things aren't going our way, it can be isolating. It's important to believe in the vision and have trust in our leaders. I often get on my knees, and cry out to God, "Lord, you know how I feel." The great thing is that I know my senior leaders are doing the same thing. I'm not alone. Everyone I serve with on the team knows we're not perfect, but together, we're going to God to refine us.

A turning point came in my leadership when I realized I had become an island when it came to decision making. In our Washington launch, we had not trained our leaders to make decisions for themselves, but since we had to make them quickly, I tended to make them all myself. I was becoming a bottleneck. I had to go back and release the leaders on my team to lead on their own and give them permission to fail. I grew in my leadership when I learned to establish seasons of lengthening the leash, incorporating wisdom and trust. When you are a shallow leader, you tend to make all the decisions alone. A deeper leader develops others.

I think the biggest lesson I've learned as a leader is to not hesitate. It was always my tendency to wait and craft my thoughts before speaking them, but I've learned to act quickly and in confidence. I don't give myself time to second-guess myself. There's a tension between acting quickly and processing, and I've learned to manage it by leaning into the mentorship of other great leaders and asking myself some important questions, such as, "Are there pieces of information I'm leaving behind or blowing by?" I was intimidated early on in executive meetings and spent seasons as a listener and learner. But I learned there has to come a time when you step into a godly confidence based in biblical humility.

A huge lesson came through a hard conversation with one of my pastors. After keeping my ideas to myself in a team meeting, he challenged me as to why I was there. He said, "Linda, you were brought here for your good thinking, so bring it. If you can't, you don't belong here." This was a hard conversation, but I took it to heart. I've learned to check my feelings at the door. I may get shot down, but that's okay. I've come to trust the pastors in this group, just as they've come to trust me. They were patient, willing to give me the time and space to develop if I was willing to learn and take risks. That was a big question, and I've had to ask myself if I really felt God calling me to this level of leadership. If so, I needed to have the courage to be vulnerable and put myself out there.

PRINCIPLES TO GROW ON

Linda's story and my own both illustrate that isolation is a common hurdle in leadership. Perhaps as you read Linda's story you might be thinking, *Well, sure, she had an executive team that encouraged her gifts and helped her develop, but what if I don't?* It's a good question, so let's answer it. One of the principles I've learned is that isolation is Satan's plan. You can't afford to buy in to the lie that there's no one out there to lean on to help you grow. Satan doesn't want you to reach out beyond your cone of silence to ask for help. He wants you to suffer alone, hoping you'll never attempt to use your leadership gifts or develop them. He wants you to see your gender and age as roadblocks. They are neither. Lift up your eyes beyond your current circumstances and seek out someone a little wiser, a little farther down the leadership road, and offer to buy that person a cup of coffee. Then pick his or her brain!

ENCOURAGEMENT AND CHALLENGE

Along the way, I've learned to lean in to two kinds of people: encouragers and challengers. The encouragers always have kind, affirming words for you that refresh you and keep you going, kind of like enjoying a cold glass of milk and a warm cookie at Grandma's after a hard day at school. These are the people who see your gifts and strengths and call them out to encourage you in your lowest moments. I have one such friend, Sibyl, who lives several states away, but in some of my most desperate moments, God uses her to pick up the phone and speak into my heart. With a voice like Carol Channing, she says my name, and I can hear the smile in her voice. Although she's far away, her words make it feel as if her arms are wrapped securely around me. Her timing is always impeccable and affirms in my heart just how much God loves me.

The challengers always make you think further, work harder, and push us to grow into all that we can be, like Bob, the personal trainer at the gym. He sometimes barks, and often his words are hard to hear, but they always help me grow to that next level. I've had various challengers in my life and have learned to grow from them even when their words or personality rubbed me the wrong way. One of the keys here is to shut down the defensiveness that threatens to rear its ugly head. Admit what you don't know. Listen for truth. Take on the attitude of a learner, and lean in hard to the wisdom that will come your way.

You need both encouragers and challengers in your life, and while sometimes their presence may not be immediately apparent to you, they are there. To find them, look around and ask yourself a few questions: Who knows me well and has a comforting, encouraging presence I can sink into? This encourager needs to be another woman with a strong love for Jesus who can speak words of affirmation into your soul. For potential challengers, ask, "Who has leadership gifts I admire that I can learn from? Who is strong in areas that I'm weak in?" Look for someone grounded in biblical principles and humility that will speak words of truth into your life and open your mind to those outside your usual circle or vocation.

To take advantage of both types of people in my life, I've learned to keep a leadership journal, savoring the nuggets of wisdom people share with me: quotes, key conversations, recommended books and articles, and encouragement. I used to keep these tucked in the back of my Bible scribbled on whatever paper I could find, but it got out of control. I decided I didn't want to explain to God why my Bible resembled a rat's nest, so I've now resorted to a notebook.

SO WHAT ABOUT YOU?

We were created to live in community. Hebrews 10:25 reminds us of this: "Don't give up the habit of meeting together; instead let us encourage one another." God created us with the need to lean into him and to others. Ask God to send those encouragers into your life and for the courage to be vulnerable and admit when your encouragement tank is running low. God also reminds us in Proverbs 27:17, "As iron sharpens iron, so one person sharpens another." Ask God today to send the challengers you need and the wisdom to seek their input. It takes courage, but God is here to help. Trust in the words of Jeremiah 29:11: "For I know the plans I have for you, declares the Lord. These are plans to prosper you, not to harm you but plans to give you a hope and a future." In this verse, God reminds us that he not only thinks about us but has plans for us bigger than we've ever dreamed of. He goes on to say he's always home with the light on, and if we come knocking, we'll find the help we need.

Start today by spending time in God's Word, listening to his clear, calm voice, and leaning into both the encouragers and challengers he's placed in your path.

QUESTIONS FOR REFLECTION AND DISCUSSION

1. How do you handle the isolation and loneliness of leadership? Are there particular times of leadership when you feel most alone? Why do you think this is?
2. Do you feel your age or gender are isolating factors? If so, what's your plan to overcome this?
3. Do you have both encouragers and challengers in your life? What are the biggest lessons you've learned from them? If not, do you have a list of names to pray over as potential candidates for these roles?

CHAPTER 2

I'M NOT AFRAID

It's interesting that I (Sherry) am writing this chapter on fear as I sit strapped to my seat inside a big metal bullet that feels as if it was shot from a cannon. In case that description wasn't clear, I am on a plane that just took off in the middle of a windstorm in Orange County, California. We're not talking about the type of wind that ruffles the hairdo you just worked on for thirty minutes. No, these are hurricane-force winds that could strip the fur off a bearcat before he even had the chance to scratch your eyes out. It's been on the news all day. I'm gripping the edge of my seat and hoping the pilot is not up there in the driver's seat crying like a twelve-year-old girl, which is what I feel like doing.

As we bounce around though the clouds, I'm reminded again that I willingly signed up for this. I bought my ticket, I boarded the plane, I buckled up, but now I have no control. Digging my nails into the armrest and tightening my seatbelt isn't going to make the plane fly smoothly. My safety and that of my fellow travelers is now in the hands of the pilot. Crazy thoughts are running through my head. "Has he flown through a windstorm before?" "What if he can't read the controls because we're bouncing around so much?" "Did I check to see if I smelled alcohol on anyone's breath as I passed by the cockpit, and did the pilot look old enough to shave?"

My husband sitting next to me is cool as a summer cucumber. He tried to say something to me, but I couldn't answer. I feel paralyzed, and all I can think about is getting back on terra firma.

This is what fear does. It sends our heart rate through the roof, takes our once-rational thinking in crazy directions, and shuts us down when it gets out of control. It can be a horrible "get me out of here" feeling.

As I'm sitting here, I'm asking myself, *What am I really afraid of?* Well, for starters, falling out of the sky and crashing into the mountains below, my body exploding in a million bits. Okay, maybe that's not going to happen. But how long is this turbulence going to go on, and how bad is it going to get? These are things I don't know and won't know until we've passed through this storm. It's the unknown and the fact that I don't have control over it that scares me.

Have you ever had those moments in leadership? You faced a situation where you desperately wished you could see into the future and how it would turn out. For most of us, the new and unknown has a unique ability to throw us into a tailspin. Uncertainty is like a free pass for my imagination to run amok. And instead of my thoughts turning to the good and the beautiful as Philippians 4 suggests, mine tend to seek a downward slide into the pit of panic. Isn't it just as possible that things will go well instead of disastrously? And in some cases, isn't a positive outcome even more likely? That the rough air will change to smooth and the plane will eventually land safely? Of course. Again, I have to ask myself the question, *What am I really afraid of?*

As I sit here on the plane, I'm staring straight into the face of a leadership opportunity where the unknown looms large. The reason I'm on this flight is that my husband and I are relocating to a new city where I will begin a new job. Actually it's not just a new job, but a totally new calling, into a career that is a tremendous opportunity, both exciting and daunting. As I sit here, I have to confess to dealing with thoughts of fear and uncertainty. What if they don't like me? What if this job isn't a good fit? What if I face situations that are bigger than me? My fears point to the fact that what I'm afraid of is failure, letting others and myself down, of having to admit my weaknesses and areas of inadequacy. Kind of smacks of pride, doesn't it?

A big question I often wrestle with is what God wants me to do with fear. In the Bible, we find references to it. In fact, God instructs us to fear him, as explained in the words of the prophet Jeremiah: "Should you not fear me? declares the Lord. Should you not tremble in my presence?"

As I read these words, I know that God isn't telling me to dread him or avoid him the way we'd keep our distance from something scary or dangerous. He's gently reminding us of who he is: the all-powerful Creator of the universe.

I know God is all powerful, but what do I do when I'm terrified, when I'm feeling the gut-wrenching kind of fear that stops me cold? Research shows us that sometimes fear can be healthy and work for good. In situations where there is real danger, your body does a number of things automatically so it's ready for quick action or a quick escape. Your heart rate increases to pump more blood to your muscles and brain. Your lungs take in air faster to supply your body with oxygen. Your pupils get larger so you can see better. And the systems in your body slow down temporarily so you can concentrate on more important things. Fear can make you stop before jumping into something dangerous or foolish, like jumping off a bridge or stepping in front of a car. It can send alarm signals to your brain that you need to go in another direction or seek help, as in the case of walking down a deserted street alone or when you are lost. It can save you from a hasty decision by making you pause, giving time for wisdom to prevail. It can cause your heart to cry out to God.

There's no doubt that fear can be healthy, but left unchecked, it can derail your leadership. In my own life, I've seen three different directions my fear will lead me: in, out, or up.

GOING IN

The most common direction for me is to go inward, internalizing the fear. This is where I don't tell anybody what's scaring me and go for the big cover-up. While the thoughts boil inside and loom larger and larger, I keep pretending I've got it all under control. But since I'm leaving my thoughts and fears to their own devices, they take on a life of their own, and a simple fear quickly turns into a potential disaster. If I don't make the right decision in that meeting, I'll lose the confidence of my team and get fired. It will cause such stress in my marriage that my husband will lose his job. We'll lose our house and be out on the street. Without a house, I won't be able to wash my hair or take a bath or have clean clothes. Whew! I should be up for an Academy Award with all that drama.

When I go inward with my fear, I shut down and lose access to rational thought. Since I'm not expressing my thoughts to anyone else and keeping them hidden, they seem bigger than life, like the floating balloon characters in the Macy's Thanksgiving Day Parade. This is exactly what Satan wants. He wants me to stay isolated and alone and blow things out of proportion. The times I've paid attention to this and simply put words to my fear, expressing it to a trusted colleague or a friend, I get immediate perspective.

Going inward with my fear is my first natural reaction. I think it's the most destructive.

GOING OUT

Another path I've seen myself take is to project my fear outward. This one's ugly: your fear makes you feel trapped like a caged animal and stirs up defensiveness and the inclination to lash out.

When my daughter Brittainy was in third grade, she desperately wanted a dog. Being ever frugal parents, we visited the nearest animal shelter where she immediately fell in love with a golden retriever/chow mix named Mufasa. The name quickly degenerated down to Moose, which wasn't just easier to say; it fit him. He was a lumbering seventy pounds of hairy bad breath, and despite his size, he was neurotic and scared of his own shadow. He spent his first few days with us with his big hairy backside wedged into the corner of our dining room, growling or flinching every time my husband walked by. His message was clear: *I'm afraid. I don't trust you! Stay back!* It took a few days, but he began to relax and then took to the habit of plopping his big self on our feet every time we sat down, as if to anchor us in place.

As a leader, have you ever felt backed into a corner by your fear, with defensiveness threatening to take over? Taking this route can cause you to be suspicious of others, be overly protective of your territory, and become autocratic, throwing edicts around like confetti at a parade. It can affect not only your work performance but your family and friendships, because as they see you spiraling off in this direction, they tend to back off in self-defense.

When I'm in this mode, I start to power up. I feel the need to do something, anything, about the situation that's causing me fear, but I don't know exactly what to do, and I lash out. The rare times I've been able to catch myself doing this or someone else has been brave enough to point it out, I'm reminded to slow down. Just as Moose needed a few days to chill out in our dining room, I sometimes need to take a few minutes (or hours) to bring my thoughts and emotions back down to a reasonable level.

GOING UP, THE BEST DIRECTION

I have to believe that neither of these paths is the one God wants for me. He wants me to go up. The Bible tells me that God wants to know me; in fact in some versions, it uses the word *desperate*. He craves for me to bring my thoughts, joys, and fears to him so he can know every part of me. I know he wants me to go up with my fear, but why is this so often my last resort? It often feels to me as if I shouldn't be experiencing fear in the first place. There's an element of shame behind the fact that things scare me, and in my leadership, I'm sometimes terrified. I often tell myself, "Oh, grow up!" as if being afraid is a lack of maturity or the result of being a ninny. The truth is, we all face it. From the president of the United States to the mom at home figuring out how to best lead her family, we all face those moments of scary decisions and uncertain paths. And God wants us to come to him—actually run to him with this, even when we're ashamed of it. I love the words in Isaiah as God comforts the children of Israel in their fear: "Do you ever feel like a lowly worm, Jacob? Don't be afraid. Feel like a fragile insect, Israel? I'll help you. I, God, want to reassure you. The God who buys you back, the Holy of Israel" (Isaiah 41:14).

I love those words: "the God who buys you back." I get to run to a God who went to limitless lengths to rescue me. He loved me so much that he sought me out. And when I run to him with my fear, it exposes me to the truth and allows me to relax because I've relinquished control to the one who loves me most. It helps take my eyes off my immediate circumstances and leads to a sense of peace about the future.

Big Transitions

I first experienced the power of this when I moved from administration in a public school to being a staff member at a large multisite church directing the children's ministry. I entered with confidence. After all, I had lots of experience. In the education world, I had led teams of teachers and oversaw curriculum for more than a thousand students.

But I quickly learned that children's ministry is quite different from a public school. For starters, the kids weren't required to come; they chose to come. They weren't there to simply learn; they were there to experience God and what a relationship with him could be. Most of the leaders were volunteers; the motivation of a paycheck didn't even enter the picture. They served out of their passion to see kids come to Christ. All the foundations that I knew flew out the window: standardized test scores, teacher evaluations, attendance reports, curriculum requirements. My new job quickly distilled down to one central question: How could we best come alongside children and families to help them see Jesus as their forever friend and Savior? As I realized the enormity of the job, I began to feel a sense of fear. I was in new territory and didn't know what I was doing. Big things were at stake.

Help came in the form of one of my team members, a former teacher who gently prompted me to relax with the corporate approach and go up to God. We spent time praying as a team, sharing scriptures from our own quiet times that we felt God wanted us to pay attention to. We focused with laser vision on bringing Christ to the kids and parents in a real, relevant way.

Big Lessons

Here's what I learned from this experience: it's tempting to focus on what you can control to build your own sense of security. You can build spreadsheets of numbers and statistics, and you can lean into processes and theory, all of them good things. But when you've reached the end of yourself and leadership fear is looming large, the only sure source for help is up. And this is where you have the raw, honest conversation: "God, I admit I don't know what I'm doing. I need your wisdom and direction and divine inspiration, because I sure can't do this on my own." God's answer from Isaiah 41 is simple: "I'll help you."

Elisa's Story

I recently asked my friend Elisa Morgan, who served as the first CEO of MOPS International (Mothers of Preschoolers) and saw a fledgling organization grow to connect and support 100,000 moms spread across the United States and throughout the rest of the world, to share her leadership story. When I asked

Elisa about the times she's experienced fear most in her leadership, she shared these thoughts.

❖

I have been "most" afraid many times! All were when I lost perspective on what was up to me and what was up to God. When I took the position of CEO of MOPS International, I was terrified. It seemed to me that everyone else in a position of leadership surely knew what they were doing. But I didn't! I'd never been a CEO before. At times I overfunctioned. I took too much responsibility for everything: how the board led, what to do in a personnel crisis, whether to shift our mission statement.

Over time I recognized that God often invites us into experiences where we've never before set foot. When he does, it's up to us to not become overly responsible but rather to yield what we have and what we don't have to God and ask him to make both enough. Personally I've often said, "My deficits have become my offering." God is faithful to make something out of little. But also I've learned that while God uses both successes and mistakes to shape us, he also uses them to shape those with whom we serve, as well as the mission to which we are called. I've come to believe that in some situations, this "underground" growth is actually more important to God than the outcomes we've been focused on.

Even after years of experience, I still deal with fear often. I find it's easy to forget what I've learned, especially when the circumstances change. Today I lead a solo life, speaking and writing and mentoring on my own. In this season of leadership, I look around, and the memorials of past learning are less present. No office, no staff, no team: it's up to me to remember how God has provided in my past when I face new challenges. I think many women fall into the trap I fell into: thinking that everyone else knows what they're doing and that everyone else is confident and equipped. The reality is that we're all in need of God's wisdom and power to respond to whatever we face in a given moment. We're not enough. We never will be. But God chooses to invite us all to participate in influencing through leadership. He will make our "not enough" enough.

PRACTICAL WAYS OF DEALING WITH FEAR

As Elisa so eloquently shared, fear is part of leadership, and everyone experiences it. So what will you do with yours? Here are some practical ways I've learned to make sure I'm going up with my fears.

Bring It into the Light

Satan wants you to keep your fear secret so he can make it look bigger than it is. In my life, this leads to worry and causes me to obsess about the problem. An easy way to address this is to give it a name—for example, "I'm concerned about this upcoming meeting because it could uncover some uncomfortable tension." Listen to yourself as you name it, making sure you aren't blowing it out of proportion: "I'm scared about this upcoming meeting because if we expose this tension, it will poison the whole team and ruin the project."

Now find a trusted advisor or mentor outside the situation to talk about your fear. Be honest about what you're afraid of, even if it makes you look like a scaredy-cat. Ask for that person's perspective about the situation, remembering to focus on your feelings and doubts, not the actions or character of the people involved. As you talk it over, listen to your words and remind yourself it isn't a disaster, but something to be thought about with calm reason.

This worked for me on the plane out of Orange County. After about ten minutes, I turned to my husband and said, "This turbulence is bad. I don't like it." Just saying this out loud made me feel better and not so panicky. I had now relegated this tremendous windy mess down to a little word: *turbulence.* My husband's response, "Yeah, it'll pass in a few minutes," made me realize I was going to be okay.

Form a Prayer SWAT Team

A few years ago, I had the privilege of leading a collaborative group of women church executive leaders. These women were brilliant and fearless, often leading under tremendous pressure. One of them shared a situation where she felt under spiritual attack, initiated by a woman in her church congregation. It became apparent that this person had been undermining her leadership, talking behind her back, and spreading untruths to anyone who would listen. This leader's response was stellar. She admitted to feeling fear and anxiety and quickly formed what she termed a prayer SWAT (special weapons and tactics) team. She sought out trusted friends she could count on to bathe the situation in prayer, and I was privileged to be part of the team. Periodically, I would receive e-mails from her; they never contained gossip about the misguided woman, but instead asked us to petition God for wisdom to respond in gentleness and love. When the e-mails came, all of us would immediately stop and pray and then reply with encouragement and reminders that God was indeed in control. Though the SWAT team wasn't formed for me, I was tremendously encouraged when I read the replies. This leader already knew what I was just beginning to learn: when you have godly friends, you need not go through hard situations alone.

Attack the Worry Monster

It's true that the best defense is a great offense. Worry feeds fear, and instead of letting the worries and fears snowball, how about launching a counterattack? God's all for nipping worry in the bud, as he points out in Philippians 4:6–7: "Don't fret or worry. Instead of worrying, pray. Let petitions and praises shape your worries into prayers, letting God know your concerns. Before you know it, a sense of God's wholeness, everything coming together for good, will come and settle you down. It's wonderful what happens when Christ displaces worry at the center of your life."

A wise mentor shared with me her secret to launching a counterattack on the worry monster. She found key verses, such as Philippians 4, that reminded her of God's power over her circumstances. She wrote them down, posted them where she'd see them often, and then turned her worry into wonder by relinquishing ownership of her specific fears. She'd pray, "God, this problem is yours now. I can't wait to see what you are going to do with it!" Voilà! The burden lifted from her shoulders, replaced with the freedom that comes with complete trust.

Get Help with a Few Reminders

Even when you consistently go up with your fear, do you find yourself sliding back into the old habits of worry or needless anxiety? There's nothing more helpful than a loving reminder that stops you mid-descent, before the grip of fear has taken hold. Give a trusted friend permission to call you out when he or she sees you succumbing to fear or worry. Are you letting fear creep into your words? Are you withdrawing or attempting a master cover-up? Are you sliding into attack mode? Allow that friend to gently call your attention to your words and actions and then, with humility, listen and take action.

GOD IS BIGGER

As a children's pastor, I loved it when a great object lesson or word picture came along that allowed me to relate God's power to the children. One such lesson came wrapped up in the song "God Is Bigger Than the Boogie Man," by Veggie Tales.[1] The song starts with Bob the Tomato cowering in his bed, because he's afraid of the dark and sees all kinds of scary things. It then launches into a reminder that God is bigger than anything we can think of, real or imagined. He's bigger than Godzilla or the monsters on TV, and he's bigger than any leadership problem we'll ever face. The song ends by reminding us that no matter how big or terrifying the situation is, God can handle it.

How true. God *can* handle it, and he wants to see me succeed as a leader. No matter how difficult the situation or how big the decision, as long as I'm holding God's hand, I'm going to be okay.

QUESTIONS FOR REFLECTION AND DISCUSSION

1. When do you feel the most afraid in your leadership? Have you asked yourself what you are really afraid of?

2. When you feel threatened or afraid, do you tend to go in, out, or up? Are there strategies you've found that help you to remember to go up?

3. Do you have a circle of godly friends to help you attack the worry monster? What other strategies help you overcome worry?

CHAPTER
3

THE MONSTER YOU ARE AVOIDING

I (Sherry) remember exactly where I was sitting on the bed when I asked my mom the question. As was customary on a Saturday night, I was decked out in my pink pajamas and quilted robe as my mom rolled my hair up in little cylinders of torture, otherwise known as curlers. If you were born anywhere near the 1960s, you know exactly the ones I refer to. They were bristly as steel-wool pads, with evil tentacles that tangled obstinately in my long hair. To add insult to injury, they were held in place with little plastic spikes that left tiny craters in my scalp. After all the curlers were in place, a hairnet was applied in case I encountered hurricane-force winds while lying in bed, or maybe it was to keep my wily fingers from unwinding the hateful things before they had time to work their magic. The question, and it was a serious one for a seven year old, was, "Mom, do you think I'm pretty?"

My mom, without skipping a beat replied, "Of course, I do. Now hold your head still so we can get this finished." My mom wasn't being insensitive; she was concentrating on the short window of time for curler completion before I wiggled off the bed. She had no way of knowing that what I was really asking was, "Do I measure up to all the other girls? Is there anything special about ME?"

You see, that very day, I had encountered Jeffrey. He lived two doors down, and we had always played together. He never seemed

35

to mind too much when I beat him in four square, but this time as I approached ready for a game, he looked me right in the eye and said, "You're ugly and stupid, and you're not playing with me today." I will never know if Jeffrey's mom had slipped a big scoop of mean into his corn flakes that morning, but I shuffled away feeling stunned, confused, and focused with laser acuity on the word *ugly*.

As I sat on my mom's bed that evening, I caught a glimpse of myself in the bureau mirror. My heart sunk: Jeffrey was right. I looked stupid in my pink quilted bedtime ensemble, and my head looked like something that belonged in a science-fiction movie. My teeth gapped in the front, and my eyelashes didn't flutter like those of the girl who sat in front of me in school whose name sounded like an island in Hawaii. Was I pretty? I wasn't feeling it, and I had Jeffrey to back me up.

Unfortunately, most women have had a similar childhood experience. It may not have been a run-in with the word *ugly*, but maybe it was a party you got excluded from or a remark from a teacher or parent, and suddenly your confidence drained away like the last of the Saturday night bath suds.

That same feeling follows us into adulthood as we ask ourselves, *Am I smart enough? Do I have enough education for this position? Do I have the experience that this job demands?* The questions may change as we get older, but they all point to one lurking monster that may feel as if it's getting bigger by the minute: insecurity. Insecurity can hit you unexpectedly. One minute, you're feeling pretty cool and together, and then wham! You're left with sweaty palms asking some pretty big, unsettling questions. *Am I enough? Can I measure up? Do I have what it takes? Do I even belong here?*

THE BOTTOMLESS PIT

These questions can start to snowball, taking us deeper and deeper into the insecurity monster's lair. With me, it starts with comparisons. My hair looked okay until I saw the way that blonde girl had hers fixed. I thought my kids were doing well in school until my best friend told me about her darling superstars. My answer sounded okay coming out of my mouth until my colleague spoke up, making my response sound half-baked. I was proud of the progress of my team until I heard the reports from the other team leaders.

How is it that we can know in our heart of hearts that we have to play for an audience of only one, but then feel so crummy in the light of others' accomplishments? Could it be that we start believing what we're feeling? We feel less than what we ought to be when we're lined up against someone else, and so, we figure, it must be true that we are less.

Let's dissect that for a moment under the microscope of reality. Our feelings are big fat liars that will turn on us in a skinny minute. They comprise strong, powerful emotions that are sometimes wonderful and euphoric. But when it comes to supporting the facts, they are as flimsy as the wet lunch napkin you wiped your mouth on. As leaders, we can't afford to be held captive by something fed by a source so fleeting and changeable.

Sometimes our insecurity can be fed by something outside our own head. Just as I was influenced by young Jeffrey, who probably had woken up on the wrong side of the bed that day, we can also be steered in dangerous directions by the voices and opinions of others. Have you ever had someone criticize your work? Question your decisions? Point out your lack of experience? Or just flat out not like you? Of course. We all have. It isn't this experience that separates the great leaders from the mediocre; it's how they react to it that is so refining. What do you do when you face disparaging comments, whether well intentioned or mean-spirited? Do you take them out and examine them in the light of truth to see what you can learn, or do you immediately let them wound your spirit? Do you search these comments for wisdom, or let them seep in as discouragement that feeds your insecurity?

I have a friend who is bright and talented, but she often gets led astray with the words and opinions of others. The other day, she was excited about a new idea she had, but when I saw her twenty-four hours later, she was discouraged and not talking about the idea at all. When I asked why, she said two people on her team thought that the idea would never work. Her excitement and confidence from the day before now turned to uncertainty, which led her down the thought path of insecurity. She was saying things like, "They're probably right; it's a dumb idea. I didn't really know what I was talking about." All of this because someone had disagreed with her! God urges us not to be so easily persuaded by others' opinions but to stand firm in him. I love the way James 1:5–8 encourages us:

> If you don't know what you're doing, pray to the Father. He loves to help. You'll get his help, and won't be condescended to when you ask for it. Ask boldly, believingly, without a second thought. People who "worry their prayers" are like wind-whipped waves. Don't think you're going to get anything from the Master that way, adrift at sea, keeping all your options open.

DO YOUR LAUNDRY

I have a wise friend who says she sorts comments from others just the way she sorts laundry. She makes mental piles, just as she does with whites, colors, and delicates, but she labels them "encouragement," "wisdom," and "discard." When a critique or negative comment comes her way, she asks herself if there's even a small part that is a compliment to her leadership. Did the comment start with, "I love the way you ..." or "You did a good job, but ..." She gleefully adds these to her encouragement pile and then asks herself, "What can I learn from the hurtful part? Could it be true that my comment was rude and bossy? Did I blow past that person in the meeting and hurt her feelings? In my haste, did I make mistakes that I now need to clean up?" She invests the most time with these questions and has testified that she has learned from even the harshest of criticisms. She lays these lessons gently on the wisdom pile, like a treasured garment, often writing the lesson she wants to remember in her journal. The rest she discards freely, flinging the stinging comments back over her left shoulder like a worn-out nightgown, knowing that the less time she ponders or mentally rehashes it, the less time she's wasting. It's a brilliant solution, and no sense of security was harmed during the process!

This is a lesson I wish I had learned earlier in my leadership journey: to be grateful for the critiques and opinions of others, sifting through and learning from them and not letting them feed my insecurity. I clearly remember a wise supervisor who started teaching me this when I was a new leader of a ministry team at my church. A team member had come to ask for yet another weekend off. Knowing that her absence made everyone's job more difficult and that she had already taken more weekends off than was allowed, I said a quick no without even listening to the why of the request. My supervisor called me in and expressed his disappointment, saying I hadn't taken the time to find out if it was an important family matter that had prompted the request. He also shared some wisdom in how he often dealt with this same situation and even added some kind words about my usual leadership style, but I couldn't get past the "you screwed up" part. I walked out crushed by the fact that my team member had gone over my head and complained about me to my boss. My insecurity meter skyrocketed, and I sat in my office wondering how I had become such a rotten leader. An hour later, my supervisor called to check on me. He said, "You know, you really are doing a good job. Here's what I wouldn't stress over and here's what I think you can learn from this." He was doing my mental laundry sort for me, and I didn't even realize it.

Unfortunately, there are voices that we shouldn't waste sorting time on. These are the unhappy few who never have an encouraging word to say and leave us feeling as if our security tank had just been siphoned dry. If you have someone like this in your life, you may have to limit the time you spend in his or her company. If the negative feedback is constant, you may send this person's comments directly to the discard pile. You also need to be aware of voices that may be feeding you that are not relationships. Television programs and commercials can often make us go into a tailspin of comparison or spur negative feelings about ourselves. How come my teeth are never that white? How is it that her boss loves everything she does though she never spends a moment working? How come I eat a fat hamburger, and my stomach is not flat like that leggy model's? Yet we spend hours watching this stuff, allowing it to sink into our heads and hearts that this is what we should want, or believe, or become. Ridiculous!

THE VICIOUS CYCLE

The feelings of insecurity can be deadly to your leadership. It can leave you questioning every decision, becoming overly hesitant and overly dependent on others' thoughts or feelings. Left unchecked, insecurity can affect the core of who you are, with some significant consequences that can lead to even more insecurity. While some of us tend to retreat or withdraw when our sense of security is attacked, others take a more irritating approach: overcompensating. This can be dangerous and leave us stranded on the thin limb of false pride and arrogance.

I hate to admit it, but this is where I often find myself. If I'm not sure what my boss is thinking about me, I'll work overtime or take on extra projects. If I get caught short not knowing an answer or being ill prepared in a meeting, I'll overprepare for the next one. If I find myself in a conversation that's over my head, I have caught myself pretending to be in the know by nodding my head, agreeing to things I know nothing about. Not only is this rooted in pride and self-importance, but it's a total waste of time and utterly exhausting.

TWO PICTURES OF LEADERSHIP

As I pondered this chapter on insecurity, two friends came to my mind. Both of them are gifted leaders but with very different approaches to their own shortcomings. The first one is a talented, beautiful woman with a well-developed sense of style. As a volunteer in a church, she rose quickly into a staff leadership role, relying heavily on her natural talent and confident demeanor. As I got to know her better, though, I began to notice some cracks in her facade. She didn't lean into others and didn't expand her knowledge with outside reading or time with mentors. She once confided that she often pretended to know the answers and that it was more important that her team had the perception that she knew what she was doing than whether she really did. She was shifted to several different leadership roles, but everywhere she went, her team would soon begin to grumble, and poor morale would ensue.

My other friend never stood out in any way. She had dealt with a physical disability all her life, but after a few minutes in her presence, you didn't notice it. As a staff volunteer, she rose slowly into leadership, reading as many books on leadership as she could get her hands on, jotting notes on what she learned, and patiently putting the lessons into practice. I often saw her in coffee shops or restaurants meeting with others, leaning into their wisdom, and quietly sharing her own. Her humility and gentle sense of complete confidence in who God had made her to be stood out. She didn't have a lot of experience or notable talent, but she was a leadership magnet. I found myself drawn to her as a young leader and met with her often. When I would ask her a question that stumped her, she'd pause and without apology, say, "I have no idea, but I'm going to do some research." And she did just that. She was a humble learner who didn't let her lack of knowledge, experience, or talent get the best of her. She relied daily on the God who made her to complete her, and it showed in her every word and action.

I often stepped back and watched the reaction of others to these two friends. Although the first friend sometimes got more public attention, I saw many more drawing on the wisdom of the second, finding ways to spend time in her presence, and often seeking her out for advice or prayer. I learned valuable lessons from both of these women, but I felt drawn to emulate the habits of the second friend.

Tammy's Story

Another friend who is the perfect picture of godly confidence is Tammy Kelly, who has served as executive director at several large churches and has consulted with numerous church leaders. Through her varied experience in ministry leadership, Tammy has faced situations that were pressure filled and demanded confidence and fast thinking on her feet. I asked Tammy to share what she's learned about leading in difficult situations and overcoming feelings of insecurity.

❖

Oh goodness! No matter how bold and brave I often appear to be on the outside, I am often dealing with self-doubt on the inside. I don't think I have ever done anything that would be considered great. I just keep showing up, and somehow my steady perseverance gets transformed into confidence.

Sometimes my insecurity has evolved from being a woman in senior leadership roles in the world of church where that is not always the norm and, quite honestly, not always welcomed. Back about ten years ago, I was newly on the leadership team at Willow Creek Community Church and was invited to be part of a group of pastors from other large churches. This was a group of fifteen to twenty people that had emerged with the desire of these people to get together every six months without a formal agenda to share learning in a safe environment.

The first gathering that I attended was at South East Christian Church, and there were fifteen or so church leaders from a mix of churches: Saddleback, North Point, Cherry Hills, Southland Christian Church, and a few others. I walked into the room. There was mostly men present, but to my surprise, there was also a handful of other women. I assumed everyone was part of the invited church leadership group.

After a continental breakfast, one of the organizers of the group made an announcement: "The van to take the wives shopping has arrived. Have a good day, ladies."

Now it made sense! Some of the men had brought their wives along to enjoy beautiful Kentucky. As they filed out, I realized that I was the only woman left in the room. It was particularly awkward when one of the guys said to me, "Hey, you better hurry up. You don't want to miss your day shopping." I let him know I was actually staying for the meeting, at which point he rushed over to kindly pull my chair out for me to sit down. It was incredibly awkward.

The two-day session was great, but I was fighting insecurity the whole time, not sure what the male leaders thought of having a woman in their circle.

Six months went by, and the group was gathering again. It was such a great learning opportunity that I decided to put my insecurity aside and show up again. Of course, my confidence lasted until about two minutes before I was supposed to walk through the doors to join the group, and quickly my mind went to, "What am I doing here? They probably don't want a woman involved."

Partway through day 1, I pulled aside one of the organizers of the group, the executive pastor of Saddleback for over twenty years, and said, "Hey, if it feels weird having a girl part of this group, I totally understand. Just let me know, and I will not be offended at all."

He gave me an odd look and said, "What? I never thought about it. I just consider you one of the guys."

To make me feel better, when I was out of the room making a phone call, he had a group conversation with the other church leaders attending this gathering to see if anyone was bothered by having a woman in the group. When I walked back in, I was candidly told that I was very welcome to be part of the group and that being a woman wasn't an issue at all.

I continued to meet with that group about every six months for the next seven years. Over that time, it expanded a bit. No other women joined, but I always felt part of the troupe. I think what I learned from this is that my insecurity was exactly that: *my* insecurity.

Insecurity tends to show up in my life just as I am having the opportunity to really grow. In other words, the bigger the opportunity, the bigger my insecurity. I absolutely love a big challenge, so I am quick to say yes to the next hill to climb, but the closer it gets to the day the results are expected, the more insecure I become. Some of that has to do with just wanting to steward organizational resources and people well. I don't want to waste money or hurt people. I think that is a good thing about myself that I never want to change. Insecurity can be good if it causes you to be self-aware and pause and evaluate the opportunity carefully. Insecurity can be bad if it paralyzes you.

I think most leaders have moments and seasons of insecurity. My advice is not to get too hung up worrying about it. Many years ago, I was listening to a missionary speak about confidence and insecurity, and he said, "All you can do is all you can do, and all you can do is enough." That phrase plays in my mind often.

I don't know that I have overcome insecurity, but I have learned to plow through it. God always takes us on interesting journeys, sometimes through situations where I say, "No way can I tackle that!" But then I think back on other times when I thought, "No way," and I see that God somehow brought me through the situation. God's past success in my life gives me courage to put insecurity aside and take on the challenge.

ROUTINE AND REPETITION

Tammy's story is a reminder that our sense of security and confidence needs to come from God, and his voice should trump the voices and circumstances of our lives. We've all heard Psalm 139, which reminds us, "You are beautifully and wonderfully made," and we try hard to believe it. But how do you let these truths sink in and take root? How do you integrate them into your thinking so when comparisons or outside voices attack you, you'll not crumble? I think the keys are routine and repetition.

There's a video on YouTube that I chuckle at every time I see it. It's called "Jessica's Daily Affirmation."[1] Obviously taken by her mom, it captures the daily routine of five-year-old Jessica as she runs to the bathroom, hops up to straddle the sink, and, facing the mirror, reminds herself of what's true. From "I like my haircut" to "I can do anything better than anyone else," she energetically chants herself into the start of a great day. My favorite part is when she gives a smart little clap and announces, "I like my whole house!" before she jumps down and runs off.

What if we started every day like this with a bold look into the mirror, reminding ourselves that we are daughters of the most high King, who valued us so highly he traded the life of his son Jesus for our ransom? He thinks about us nonstop and delights in us. There is nowhere we can go to escape his love. He knows our shortcomings and doesn't care about them. He loves us extravagantly (insert a smart little clap here)! There is no comparison or outside voice that can stop Zephaniah 3:17 from being true: "The Lord your God is with you. He is mighty enough to save you. He will take great delight in you. The quietness of his love will calm you down. He will sing with joy because of you."

Imagine the power of this in your leadership and picture it: you, leading others from the confidence and grace you've acquired because you remind yourself every day who you are as God's loved and cherished daughter. Before you walk out the door of your home, you declare out loud the things that God has promised as true, and then you live them out through your leadership. Can you see it? It's a picture of a confident you, with the perfect balance of strength and humility, a woman of gentle peace who is not constantly second-guessing herself or fighting for the approval of others. You treat others fairly because you react out of the just love God has shared with you. You make decisions wisely from the abundance of God's presence in your life. You lead in confidence even under attack from others because you know God's love for you never ends. This can be you, and in fact, it is you, with the constant daily soaking in of God's promises and truths found in his Word.

The power of repetition becomes a reality when it becomes part of your daily routine to the point that these truths become part of who you are: a safe, secure leader called by God to lead.

QUESTIONS FOR REFLECTION AND DISCUSSION

1. Are there voices in your life that drain your security tank? How do you overcome their influence?
2. In her story, Tammy mentioned that insecurity tends to show up when she's facing an opportunity to grow. When do you see insecurity rear its head in your life?
3. Are there daily routines that you've put into place that help you overcome insecurity? What are they?

CHAPTER 4

YOU'RE NOT DOING IT RIGHT

Remember that day in elementary school when you walked out of the bathroom with your skirt stuck in the back of your tights? Or the day that you wore your pajamas to school and it was *not* pajama day?

I (Jenni) had one of those moments recently.

After returning to the office from a lunch meeting, one of our staff members discreetly asked me, "Jenni, what's on the back of your dress?" When I turned around, I discovered the back of my navy blue dress was splattered with white spots. And when I say splattered, I mean *s-p-l-a-t-t-e-r-e-d*! I'd been prancing around town sporting a speckled rear end. It turns out that the chair I sat in at lunch had recently been wiped down with bleach water and left enough behind to ruin my dress—and my day.

Bleach. The agent I love when I'm scouring my house and satisfyingly killing every germ in its wake had now become my nemesis. A small amount of it properly diluted kills germs, cleans, and sterilizes. Used in the wrong way, it can quickly destroy something good.

Critics are a bit like bleach. In small doses, critics can be very helpful and necessary to provide perspective to your leadership. But in concentrated amounts, they can eat you alive.

I'm sure that as a leader, you've dealt with your share of critics. (They have an uncanny way of finding you.) I've observed that our responses tend to take one of two forms:

1. We ignore critics altogether and harden ourselves against their remarks, without gleaning anything that could be helpful or important for us to learn.
2. We absorb every criticism and agonize over it.

Critics can have a functional purpose when we use them correctly, but if you constantly take them in without discernment, they will paralyze you.

So how do we discern the value of criticism we receive? When is it helpful, and when is it plain hurtful? Is it sharpening your calling or purpose? Does it distract you or keep you on focus?

I love this quote from President Theodore Roosevelt:

> It is not the critic who counts; not the man who points out how the strong man stumbles, or where the doer of deeds could have done them better. The credit belongs to the man who is actually in the arena, whose face is marred by dust and sweat and blood, who strives valiantly; who errs and comes short again and again; because there is no effort without error and shortcomings; but who does actually strive to do the deed; who knows the great enthusiasm, the great devotion, who spends himself in a worthy cause, who at the best knows in the end the triumph of high achievement and who at the worst, if he fails, at least he fails while daring greatly. So that his place shall never be with those cold and timid souls who know neither victory nor defeat.[1]

Criticism. It's perhaps the scariest part of leadership, and it's unavoidable. By our sheer willingness to step up and lead, we've positioned ourselves in the center of the bull's-eye or the center of the arena, as President Roosevelt so descriptively suggests. It's only a matter of time before people start firing. Remember the laundry sorting tool that Sherry taught us in chapter 3? You'll need that tool for sorting the critics' voices as well. I wish I could tell you that criticism rolls right off me—that it doesn't affect me and I don't even flinch at it. But that would be anything but true. In fact, there have been some seasons of my life where criticism has held me back, made me second-guess everything I believed as a leader, and nearly caused me to walk away. There have been days when I couldn't help but wonder, *Is it really worth it?*

My guess is that you have had these days too. Anything worth doing will often be viewed as something worth criticizing.

So why does criticism sting so much?

IT'S PERSONAL

It's often the things that are a bit out of the ordinary that seem to draw the most fire. Unfortunately I've found this to be true as a woman in leadership, especially in Christian leadership. Part of what causes others to throw darts is their preconceived ideas, misperceptions, poor information, and ignorant bias about women in general. Not everyone views women in leadership through such a murky lens, and the last thing I want to do is put an unnecessary target on your back or convince you one is there when it really isn't. However, we would be remiss if we didn't acknowledge that sometimes our gender makes the target a bit bigger. Your culture and context will dictate how much that is true. In any case, leadership positions you for criticism, and how you handle it speaks volumes to others about your strength as a leader.

When I came on staff at Cross Point, we were still a relatively small church but growing quickly. Our lead pastor, Pete Wilson, and his wife, Brandi, graciously opened their home once a month for "Discovering Cross Point," our introduction class for new-comers. We staff loved these meetings. They were casual and cozy because of the Wilsons' hospitality, and they were a great way to meet people who were new to the church.

One particular evening as the meeting was winding down, I noticed a gentleman over in the corner talking intently with Pete.

He was speaking in hushed tones, and I was getting the picture that I wasn't intended to hear the conversation. I went about my business of saying good-byes to people as they were leaving and began tidying up the clutter from a night of community and good conversation. Every good church meeting includes its share of cookie crumbs and empty red plastic cups.

The gentleman who was talking to Pete left a bit later with his very meek and quiet wife. They nodded to me as they said their good-byes and walked out. Of course, curiosity got the best of me, so I asked Pete, "What was that all about?" With an obvious desire to be sensitive to me, he replied, "Cross Point is probably not the best fit for them." He paused for a few seconds, then continued when I prompted him to finish: "He doesn't believe women should be allowed to lead."

The unspoken was obvious: this couple would not be returning to Cross Point because of me. He didn't believe that I should be allowed to lead in ministry at the level and to the degree that I was leading as executive director.

I left that evening with a bit of an ache in my heart. *God, I don't understand. I believe you've called and gifted me to lead, and yet by doing the very thing that I feel you've called me to, not only me but Cross Point and its leadership are being judged and criticized.* I wrestled with concern of whether I was the right person for this job. If people were going to choose not to attend because of me, was I in the way of the ministry that God had called Cross Point to? Was it wrong for me to continue on if this could be a stumbling block for some people?

Criticism is personal, or at least we make it personal. Some of you probably think after reading that story, "Well, he just has an issue with women. It wasn't your fault, Jenni." And, yes, I know that to be true, but it is difficult not to take that type of rejection personally. If I had been a man, there would not have been an issue. And what's worse, there was absolutely nothing I could do about it. Gender-based criticism is painful because it causes me to question the very core of my identity.

There have been days where I've literally questioned God if he accidently mixed up the chromosomes at my conception. *Did you mean to put the leadership gift with the female chromosome? Surely not God? I mean you inspired what Paul wrote, right? I still don't understand why you've allowed there to be so much confusion about gender roles throughout the New Testament. Couldn't you have settled this for us a bit more? It sure would make things a lot easier for me now. Oh, yeah: part of this is the mess we created with free will and our sinful nature. You didn't mess up gender roles. We did by the choices we made and the consequences of sin continue to affect our ability to "dwell together in unity" (Psalm 133:1).* "There is neither Jew nor Gentile, neither slave nor free, nor is there male and female, for you are all one in Christ Jesus" (Galatians 3:28). *That's your heart.*

IT EXPOSES OUR ISSUES

One of the painful but constructive things criticism does is that it forces us to come to terms with some conditions that may be festering in our lives. Criticism can help us uncover some areas where there is a lack of emotional health. I've noticed in my own life that I tend to perceive criticism when it concerns the things that I am also the most vulnerable about. For example, I have a disproportionate need for affirmation. I can misplace my worth as an individual in the things that I do, therefore finding my self-confidence in accomplishment. You can imagine what happens when my accomplishments are criticized. If a project doesn't turn out as I planned and someone I respect or admire questions or criticizes it, my self-worth comes crashing down. Rather than appropriately attributing the criticism to the issue, I assign the criticism to me personally.

Shame

I've often wondered why other women leaders I've observed and I lead from a defensive posture. Many times I find myself emotionally suiting up for battle when I'm preparing for a leadership moment. Through some godly counseling I discovered that I was dealing with a much deeper issue: shame.

Brene Brown in her book *The Gifts of Imperfection* defines *shame* as "the intensely painful feeling or experience of believing that we are flawed and therefore unworthy of love and belonging."[2] When we're wrestling with issues of belonging, we're going to have difficulty leading effectively. If you still carry a subconscious concern about whether being a woman leader is wrong, your leadership is going to constantly be inhibited by this sense of shame.

Brown goes on to say, "Shame is all about fear. We're afraid that people won't like us if they know the truth about who we are, where we come from, what we believe, how much we're struggling."

When I'm bound by shame, any bit of criticism feels like an attack on who I am. Because of deep feelings of being flawed or unworthy, we are unable to discern criticism in a healthy way.

One of the most dangerous things we as women leaders do is try to cover up our shame. Often the arenas we lead in push us to put on our happy face and cover up our fears, insecurities, and inadequacies. We convince ourselves that if we don't have it all together or show any imperfection, we will lose both our influence and our opportunity to lead. But this cycle continues to perpetuate our lack of emotional health and hinders our leadership along the way.

Rejection

Criticism is personal because at our core, we fear rejection. We long to be accepted and spend a good deal of our lives trying to perform for and please others. That's why that couple's decision not to attend our church because I was a woman in leadership was so painful. They rejected me, and there was nothing I could do about it. I couldn't perform my way out of it or fix it.

Fear of rejection is painful because it's criticism of who we are, of something that is unique or distinct about us. Often this fear causes us to try to cover up something essential about how God has created us or who he has created us to be. When we become controlled by the fear of rejection, we begin to reject ourselves.

Failure

Most of us are terrified of failing. Here's the good and bad news: you're going to fail, you're not always going to measure up to others' standards or your own most of the time, and you won't always be good enough.

Fear of failure boils down to criticism of what we do. For those of us with performance-based identity issues, this fear eats at our core. If we have the tendency to tie our performance to our identity, any criticism that suggests we've failed can send us into an emotional tailspin. But to give into the fear of failure will rob us of the joy of accomplishing all that God has called us to. Fear of failure will paralyze us.

So how do we effectively confront shame, rejection, and failure? How do we use them constructively rather than allow them to be emotionally destructive?

First, take the focus off yourself. I've found that much of my fear of criticism circles back to the fact that I'm worried too much about me. I'm too self-focused. I'm looking for praise, acknowledgment, and acceptance from others who are just as fragile and insecure as I am. Criticism loses its power when we quit being self-focused. If you don't seek praise, you won't fear criticism.

Second, remember what's true. We are broken and flawed sinners. We are not perfect, and God does not expect us to be so. The most important thing we can do in our pursuit of living our calling as leaders is to remember what is true. In every situation that confronts our feelings of shame, rejection, or failure, we must remember what God says is true about us.

My friend and dynamic communicator Bianca Juarez said it this way:

> Peter heard the cock crow. Moses struck the rock. Jonah jumped ship. Eve bit the fruit and Adam followed. None of those pillars of biblical

narrative would ever claim to be perfect. And neither do I. I have faltered, and sadly, I will falter again. Paul encourages and reminds the Romans that there is not one person who is righteous; everyone has failed and fallen (3:10, 23). But as believers in Christ, we stand before critics as broken vessels yet claim, through His stripes we are healed (Isaiah 53:5); as piles of ash waiting metaphoric beauty, we claim He uses the base to confound the wise (1 Corinthians 1:27).

Dale Carnegie said, *Any fool can criticize, condemn, and complain, but it takes character and self control to be understanding and forgiving.* Only listen to a critic if they can be forgiving. If not, be unthwarted by their comments. Like my father always told me, to escape criticism, do nothing, say nothing, be nothing.[3]

What are you afraid of being criticized for? Take a moment and write it down. Be aware of where fear tends to paralyze you, and then remember that you are going to be the most prone to throwing in the towel and giving up when you receive criticism that confronts those fears.

DISCERNING CRITICISM: IT'S OUR CHOICE

Criticism can be constructive or destructive. It's all in what we do with it. The critic doesn't hold the power of our response. We do. He may be able to throw his darts, but he can't control their impact on us.

We're familiar with the destruction that criticism can cause, but if it is filtered in a healthy way, it can be constructive and move us along in our journey to become more God honoring in our leadership. So how do you discern the difference?

Filter It Through Prayer
Our tendency is to react to criticism and defend ourselves. There may be times when it is wise for you to clarify the truth, but whether a response is necessary or not, the best place to start is prayer:

"Do not be anxious about anything, but in everything, by prayer and petition, with thanksgiving, present your requests to God" (Philippians 4:6).

"In all your ways acknowledge him, and he will make your paths straight" (Proverbs 3:6).

"If any of you lacks wisdom, he should ask God, who gives generously to all without finding fault, and it will be given to him" (James 1:5).

Whatever the criticism you are facing, make it a matter of prayer first. This could mean carving out some time, even ten minutes, to talk to God about it. If you're like me, the criticism you received is all you can think about. When my blood is boiling over on an issue, I know that I have to make some time to allow God to focus my mind and heart. I'll often go off with my Bible, a journal, and a quiet place to gain perspective that can come only from seeking him first.

Seek Wise Counsel

In addition to prayer, you are also probably blessed with some great counselors who can be a safe sounding board for filtering criticism. They can help you discern whether there is any truth in the criticism you're processing. While everything that was said to you or about you may not be accurate, is there a kernel of truth about your character that could use some refining? A trusted, wise counselor (friend, mentor, pastor, spouse) can help you identify what's true or fair while also discerning what you need to disregard. The key to having wise counselors is that you must give them permission to speak truthfully and candidly while also being willing to receive the truth they share, no matter how painful it may be. The difference between critics and wise counselors is the spirit in which the truth is shared. Critics have no relational equity to speak into your life, while wise counselors have the influence to "speak the truth in love" (Ephesians 4:15).

Welcome Healthy Pruning

Every spring I get a little neurotic about the newly budding growth in our yard. While everyone else is raving about the beauty of daffodils and tulips, I'm freaking out about the weeds that are sprouting up and the shrubs that manage to take over the house seemingly overnight.

Last spring in a moment of crazed intensity, I pulled out my trusty electric hedge trimmers and went to work on one of the bushes that seemed to be taking over the back porch. About halfway through hacking away at it, I got to thinking, *This bush was just doing what it is designed to do. It's spring, so it's growing, budding, and blossoming at a rapid pace. And here I come with the electric trimmers and cut away all of its recent growth. Poor bush, I'm sure it hates me.*

In spite of my moment of pity, I continued on because I knew that as it continued to grow, it would fill back in and become a lovely and reasonably sized bush. Had I let it keep growing, it would have become unruly and taken over the other flowering plants around it, becoming destructive instead of constructive.

How many times do we find ourselves growing rapidly, only to have a critic come in and prune us back in a big way? We think we are growing and learning and doing all the right things, and then someone gives us criticism that is actually constructive but nevertheless deflates us. But sometimes pruning (aka criticism) may be just what we need to gain some perspective and see how we are influencing the world around us. Are we adding to and enhancing our environment, or are we just growing, sprawling, and taking over?

That's the distinction about criticism we have to learn to discern. Criticism, even maliciously delivered criticism, can sometimes give us a healthy pruning if we can see the shape it is trying to reveal.

We all need the guidance and pruning of others in our lives. Pruning is painful, but unruly, unguided growth is worse.

THE POWER OF FOCUS

My sport of choice is tennis. I love the game. During the 2009 French Open Men's Final, a crazed fan leaped over the stands and onto the courts to taunt the second-ranked world player, Roger Federer. As you can imagine, it was quite a scene. Tennis, with its air of prestige and sophistication, is not accustomed to unruly spectators. Within those few seconds, the emotions of the fans ran the gamut from gasps of fear to humorous snickers and then cheers as security tackled the man and hauled him off the court.

While this little drama unfolded, I kept my eyes on Roger. Here he was playing one of the most significant matches of his career and what appeared to be a crazed lunatic jumped out on the court after him. I marveled at his ability to stay calm, quickly collect himself, and immediately go back to the game (he won, ultimately launching him back into the number 1 seed).

That's the power of focus: it's what separates the winners from the losers, the good from the great. Focus can make or break you.

This episode reminds me of how easily we can get distracted by the taunts of the critics in our lives. Many things are vying to pull us away from the calling and mission God has given us. The most important thing you can do to overcome criticism is to remain focused on your calling. The enemy's goal is to distract you, and what better way to get you off track than to cut you down with criticism?

How are you reacting to criticism? Can you shake it off and refocus on "your game," or do you throw in the towel and give up the match? Are you allowing criticism to distract you from your calling or purpose?

"Therefore, my dear brothers and sisters, stand firm. Let nothing move you. Always give yourselves fully to the work of the Lord, because you know that your labor in the Lord is not in vain" (1 Corinthians 15:58).

God has gifted and called you for the unique role you play. He does not promise that your journey will be an easy one, and you will likely have your share of critics, but he will equip you as long as you keep your focus on him.

QUESTIONS FOR REFLECTION AND DISCUSSION

1. Do you have a tendency to take criticism personally? Is there a time or place in your leadership when you feel particularly vulnerable?
2. Do you most fear rejection (criticism of who you are) or failure (criticism of what you do)?
3. What steps can you take to begin to process criticism in a healthy way?

CHAPTER
5

GROWING PAINS

During a particularly tough season of leadership, some changes within the company that I (Jenni) worked for had stripped me of leadership responsibilities that I loved yet left me thankful to still be on the bus (forgive the overused analogy). I was relieved not to be let go in the numerous rounds of cuts that had been made as a result of a corporate merger, but I was still miserable. I felt underappreciated and misunderstood by my new leaders who didn't really know me or even what I was capable of. It seemed as if I had to prove myself all over again. It was one of the largest pieces of humble pie I've ever eaten.

For months I begged God to change my circumstances. I pouted. Some days I did the minimum amount of work. Other days I set out to prove myself in a big way. It was an emotional roller-coaster that still makes me queasy when I think about it.

The irony is that I learned more in that one year than I have in most of the rest of my leadership life. A dear spiritual mentor had given me a little red journal right before all hell broke loose in my job. I've never been much of a journaler. (I let go of that notion back in sixth grade when my nosey little sister decided to hone her first-grade phonics skills by reading every sacred word in my treasured purple and pink paisley diary. The flimsy lock was no match for her.) But in this season of turmoil at work, the red journal became a trusted friend. Tucked away in one of the side drawers of my desk, I would subtly pull it out in a moment of frustration to journal my thoughts, observations, and leadership opinions about the circumstances. I captured how I felt when leaders made decisions I didn't understand. I explained what I would do differently if put in their shoes. I prayed that God would give me wisdom for the moment if I one day found myself in similar circumstances.

That little red book became my confidant and companion through one of the most challenging times of my career. And while most of it reflects the pompous ramblings of a naive young leader who had no real idea what the leaders I criticized were dealing with, it helped me shift my perspective. It's a tool I keep learning from now that I find myself leading at different levels.

PRIDE

While I didn't recognize it at the time, this "red book" season of my life taught me a lot about the relationship between humility and growth. In many ways, my ramblings in the book expressed nothing but arrogant and ignorant assumptions. I thought I understood what it took to lead, and I was quick to criticize the older, more experienced leaders who, I felt, were doing it all wrong. In other words, my little red book became a reflection of all the pride lurking in my heart.

The adage "learning the hard way" seems to be truer than I would like to admit. I hope to learn from others' mistakes, but more often than not, I have to learn from my own.

That's what pride does. It convinces us we can do it on our own and that we don't need the counsel or support of others.

In 2011 I accepted the challenge of my friend Alece to choose one word for the year. Instead of making New Year's resolutions or goals, Alece challenged herself and others to choose one word to live by for the year. I agonized for weeks over my word. I really didn't want it to be what I knew it needed to be: *humility*. Who chooses humility? Choosing humility as my one word was akin to praying for patience! You know what happens when you do that. If you want your life to be marked by humility, you can be sure that there will be plenty of things that come your way that challenge your pride.

I had no idea what I was getting into. Pride creeps into life in the most surprising ways. Look, for example, at the lies that pride tells you.

"You Need to Be Needed"

We all long to belong; that's part of our human nature. But pride quickly distorts this natural longing for community into an entitled need for recognition. There's a fine line that our hearts cross from belonging into the dangerous territory of needy recognition.

A few months ago, I was attending a meeting that one of my staff was leading. It was a big meeting of over a hundred volunteer leaders, and our team was doing a fantastic job. They were motivating and challenging our volunteers. I should have been extraordinarily proud, but instead I found myself fighting with the voice of pride that was trying to convince me that I needed to be playing a bigger role. In a moment when I should have been proud of all that they accomplished, I was feeling small and insignificant because I wasn't needed. It's tough to not feel needed. It's difficult to watch other leaders shine and find yourself in the background. But it helps to be aware that those feelings grow out of pride that is telling us that we need to be important and robbing us of the joy of seeing others succeed.

"You're Too Good for That. That's Beneath You."

One Sunday I arrived at one of our campuses relaxed and looking forward to a day to hang out and serve with the team in whatever way they needed me. I didn't have a major commitment, and so I expected it to be an easy day. Before I took five steps inside the door, I realized that the floors were in desperate need of attention. The hallways in the kids' side of the building looked as if an explosion at a craft fair and goldfish cracker extravaganza had taken place simultaneously.

I wish I could tell you I swept those floors with great joy. I didn't. I forced a smile. I made some jokes. I told myself that this is exactly what a servant leader does, but all the while I wrestled with the feeling that this work was beneath me. I, the executive director of the organization, should not be sweeping the floors. Once again, pride was lying to my heart.

Other Lies

Those are just two examples of ways that pride lies to me and attempts to destroy humility. Some other lies that you may be tempted to believe could be:

"You deserve more [or better]."
"You've earned it."
"You're the only one who can do it right."
"They can't survive without you."

Jeanne's Story

Jeanne Stevens, a dear friend and copastor of Soul City Church in Chicago, shares her story of the impact of pride's lies on her leadership.

❖

In one of my first jobs, I had a boss I really struggled with. I think even in heaven where everything is perfect and right, God would have made sure that we did not have mansions in the same subdivision. There was always friction between us, and we had a hard time leading and making decisions together. The rest of the team could see the tension between us.

I built a wall between us because I had become resistant to his leadership. I thought I knew how to do his job better than he did, and my pride was getting in the way of me following him. In my immature view, I began to think that *he* was the problem. It finally got to a point where he called me into his office one day and said, "I think we need to find another department here for you to work in."

I was not very happy with this prospect and remember thinking, *He can't do that!* I decided that I would meet with his supervisor and talk with him about what I believed was the real problem, which of course was not me.

The supervisor was a leader I respected, and I was sure that he would see things clearly from my perspective. I appropriately painted the situation for him and explained to him that I had a better alternative to the problem. Then, with incredible amounts of tough love, he looked at me and said, "Jeanne, I think I know what would be good for you for this next season. I don't know if going to another department is the solution. My hunch is that what would be really good for you is if you go back to school."

I thought. Wow. *He must really believe in me. He must think that some more intentional development would grow my leadership skills.* And then he interrupted my naive thinking and said, "I think what you need to do is enroll yourself into the graduate school of character."

I was floored. I didn't know what to say.

He lovingly affirmed me and encouraged me and actually instilled quite a bit of belief in me in that moment, but he very clearly said, "If you continue to live like everyone else is the problem, you will never reach all that God has for you. Jeanne, if you could receive this as an invitation from God to enroll yourself into this graduate school of character and receive God's loving discipline in your life, I promise you that you will never be sorry and you will not believe how much you will grow." He then prayed for me, and that was the end of the meeting.

It was without a doubt the loving discipline of God in my life, and I knew that I had a very clear opportunity at that moment: I was either going to be receptive and walk into one of the greatest growth seasons of my life, or I would stay resistant to God's discipline and continue to nurture my pride, arrogance, blaming, and rationalization.

I chose to be receptive, and it was not easy. In fact, for while, it felt painful, but the growth that emerged in my life due to that season literally changed all areas of my life:

- My presence
- The way I interacted with people
- My openness to the Holy Spirit

- My vulnerability
- My marriage
- Friendships
- Hard edges

God's discipline was so loving.

I believe that when it comes to pride, God is looking to see if we will be receptive to his invitation to allow pride to be replaced with humility. God is looking for open, receptive leaders who are willing to humble themselves in him. Surrendering your resistance and pride will lead to greater freedom and greater influence.

These thoughts have become a blessing in my life when it comes to pursuing humility in a receptive way:

Receptive	Resistant
When I am corrected or confronted, I listen humbly and ask God to reveal the truth.	When I am corrected or confronted, I am stubborn and try to prove why the correction is not accurate.
I look for feedback and growth opportunities from trustworthy people and seek wise counsel from mentors, friends, and leaders.	I don't have a lot of people I consult or seek advice from because I don't really think there are a lot of wise people out there.
I seek to understand others before judging their intentions.	I am cynical and rarely believe that others have good intentions.

❖

Do you see how these destructive falsehoods inch into our hearts and our thoughts? Philippians 2:3 says, "When you do things, do not let selfishness or pride be your guide. Instead, be humble and give more honor to others than to yourselves. Pride's lies keep you focused on yourself instead of leading from humility in loving and serving others.

WITH HUMILITY COMES WISDOM

The irony of my choice of one word for the year was that the one I really wanted to choose was *wisdom.* But the more I prayed, the more I was convinced that God really wanted me to focus on humility. Imagine my reaction when I happened on this verse a few months into my humility journey: "When pride comes, then comes disgrace, but with humility comes wisdom" (Proverbs 11:2).

It all came full circle here. I had to start with attacking my pride. Understanding where it grips us and takes hold of our lives is critical to moving forward in humility and wisdom.

Humility leads us to grace, truth, and wisdom.

WISDOM AND HUMILITY

As leaders, one of the most precious commodities we can pray for is wisdom. We're foolish to believe that we're equipped on our own to handle the challenges that our leadership responsibilities demand from us. Reading through the book of Proverbs is something I regularly do as a way to immerse myself in God's wisdom. I resonate with the agony that I hear in King Solomon's writing as he pleads for wisdom. It feels immeasurable in a world that demands urgency. It feels as if our progress is so slow in a culture that expedites everything. So where does wisdom begin? It begins where pride ends and humility begins.

We've already explored ways to identify pride's voice in our life. Now let's look at ways to grow in humility.

One of the ways that we keep our hearts humble is by embracing a posture of continued growth, continued learning, a continuous pursuit of wisdom. It is difficult for arrogance or pride to get too much of a hold in our heart if we are constantly looking for what we need to learn in every situation.

Lifelong learning is one of the greatest keys to leadership, and yet it feels as if there must be some magical code to get to the key, let alone unlock the wisdom within. There is no magic formula. There is no key that instantly unlocks wisdom. Wisdom begins when the posture of our heart is such that we're humbly learning and growing and seeking God's truth in every circumstance. Here are the ways I've learned to keep my heart attuned to learning.

Read Ferociously

I love reading biographies of great leaders throughout history. What I always marvel at is that most of those leaders make a point of saying how much they read about leaders who came before them. In his book *Decision Points*, President George W. Bush notes that he read about Presidents Ulysses S. Grant and Abraham Lincoln, and while serving in the White House as president, he read ninety-five books in one year.[1]

Great leaders read, learn, and study everything they can. There's a strange dynamic that happens as we lead more: we never have less to do, and the more you do, the more you have to do. (That's exhausting just to think about!) I'm pretty sure we'll be fighting this tension until the day we die. So when it comes to life as a leader, the last thing we have extra of is time.

I frequently get asked, "How do you find time to read?" The simple answer is, "I don't *find* time; I *make* time." Some of my greatest moments of discovery and understanding have come when I've taken a strategic pause in my day to read. One of the books with the most impact for me has been John C. Maxwell's *The 21 Most Powerful Minutes in a Leader's Day*.[2] Maxwell takes his twenty-one laws of leadership and pairs them with a leader from scripture for a combination of proven leadership strategies with biblical and historical context. I reread this book nearly every year.

I encourage you to figure out what you enjoy reading and why, and schedule it into your week. Find a reading buddy, and make a weekly lunch date to discuss what you've read, start a small group devoted to studying biblical or historical leaders, or make a date with your comfiest chair, perfect cup of tea, and a good book. It's like therapy!

And in case you're interested, Sherry and I have listed some of our favorite leadership reading in the Resources section at the end of this book.

Seek Mentors

I hesitate to use the word *mentor* because our expectations of what this word means can often be distorted. I personally think that the perception that a mentor is an older, much wiser individual who commits to spending hours with you every week pouring his or her life into yours is not realistic. I think the best mentorship happens when you have a series of voices that speak to you in different ways.

In fact, I think it's unrealistic for one person to speak to the many different areas of your life. Many of us have had such high expectations for a mentor that every time we attempt to find one, we are grossly disappointed because the person doesn't meet our outrageous expectations.

Mentors come in a variety of different forms:

- *Peer mentor:* An individual who is in a similar stage of life as you and is passionate about growing in the same ways. Chips and salsa, Diet Cokes, a leadership book, and my dear friend Kat: this was the formula for my first peer mentoring relationship. For about five years, Kat and I met once a week for lunch and studied business books together. We invited each other to speak candidly about what we saw in each other's lives and challenged each other to grow. That season was one of my greatest times of growth as a leader.

- *Spiritual mentor:* A voice of wisdom and counsel who will challenge you spiritually. Remember my little red book? I received that from a kind, gracious woman whom I consider one of my spiritual moms. For several years, Karole led a Bible study in her home for the women of our company. Each week she personally studied and prepared to share truth from scripture that challenged and motivated us to pursue a heart after God. She invited us to share our prayer requests with her, and I know that she prayed fiercely for each one of us.

- *The mentor you'll never meet:* The mentors who write the books that speak to you and the blogs that inspire you. John C.

Maxwell has mentored me more than any other leader I know, and yet I may never meet him in person. I read nearly everything he writes, and I watch and observe his life. Although I may not get personal time with public personalities, the nature of our social media world gives me great insight into how they conduct themselves in everyday leadership situations.

- *Specialized mentor:* People in your life whom you have the opportunity to learn from if you are watching carefully. Consider the areas you need to grow in as a leader, and then identify people who excel at that characteristic. Invite them to lunch or to coffee, and take the time to ask them about what makes them shine in that area. Perhaps it's someone who is consistently joyful, or a great problem solver or strategist, or someone with outstanding people skills. Whatever the area that you see a need to grow in, find people who are great at it and learn from them.

The most important thing I've learned about mentorship is that it's much less formal than I've tried to make it. There are some seasons of my life that I reflect on and realize I had two or three great mentors pouring into my life without my even realizing it. At other times, I've been incredibly deliberate and sought out voices to influence me. My greatest advice is to be patient and flexible with these relationships. Your greatest mentoring moments may come at the most surprising times.

Make Every Moment a Learning Opportunity

For leaders, learning begins long before we've arrived in our ideal leadership environment. I remember vividly a time in my early twenties when I was working for the music company that I had dreamed of working for since I was thirteen years old. Getting a job at this company was no small feat; in fact, I quit college to take a job that paid six dollars an hour working part time for this company. Yes, call me crazy, but I was following my dream. If you asked my dad, I'm pretty sure he would tell you that it was one of the few times in my life he was concerned that I had lost all sense of responsibility. I had been a focused, disciplined kid, and to interrupt my education went against everything I ever believed.

That learning detour was probably one of the most important decisions I made in my early career. (Please note: if you are a college student, looking for an excuse to quit, THIS IS NOT IT!) It was an important detour because it taught me that growing as a leader happens in a multitude of ways. It might occur in classes or textbooks (I did finish school by attending classes online and in the evenings while I was working full time), in reading leadership and business books, through great mentors and peers, by observation, or by writing in the little red book.

Now I read that little red book with the spirit of a kinder soul who has been through bumps and bruises of leadership and recognizes that there was much my naive young leader did not know. Nevertheless, there are nuggets within that journal that remind me what it feels like to be the follower. Perhaps I am more sensitive as a leader because I captured the emotions that I felt as a follower.

Consider Continued Formal Education
Perhaps you should consider getting your next degree or taking some classes in an area of interest. Sometimes the structure of formal education can provide the discipline you need to challenge you to a new level of growth and learning.

Attend Conferences and Other Learning Environments
I am a conference junkie. I love hearing thought leaders speak. I love to disconnect from my regular routine to take a day or two and get away to a new learning environment. In his book *Wild Goose Chase*, Mark Batterson shares this formula that I have found to be so true for me: "Change of place + change of pace = change of perspective."[3] Sometimes a purposeful disconnect helps you see

things in a different way. Exposing yourself to new environments is a great way to expand your perspective.

Do you see the posture of the heart here? Being a lifelong learner challenges you to acknowledge your continuing need to grow and develop. It's a daily confrontation with pride and the fact that we haven't arrived at a final destination. It combats the arrogant assumption that we can handle it all. A heart bent toward continuous growth is one marked by humility.

QUESTIONS FOR REFLECTION AND DISCUSSION

1. How is pride holding you back from leading effectively?
2. What is the greatest lie that pride repeatedly tries to tell you?
3. What truth do you need to remember to confront that lie?
4. What steps can you take on your journey to seek wisdom?

CHAPTER
6

MAKE UP YOUR MIND ALREADY!

Cross Point (where I, Jenni, serve) celebrated its ten years of ministry with some exciting plans. We had recently purchased a building in downtown Nashville, Tennessee, that would become our new church home. The majority of the attendees were ecstatic about this news. The previous six years of our ministry we had partnered with another church in town to share its facility. It was a truly beautiful partnership, but we had outgrown it much sooner than we planned, and about half of our time there was eaten up by creative seating and parking initiatives. I'm pretty sure we violated fire codes weekly, and I know we were guilty of an illegally parked car or two (we *might* have gotten a few notices!).

Unfortunately for me, I missed a good portion of the celebration that was associated with this very important milestone in our church because I was preoccupied with numerous key decisions about the project. As executive director of the organization, navigating these kinds of initiatives is part of my core responsibilities, but no one could have prepared me for the responsibility this season carried.

Long before most others had an inkling of what was coming, our senior leadership team and I were analyzing our next steps.

Through prayer, analysis, thoughtful discussion, and a lot of determination, we were making decisions that would affect the trajectory of our organization for years to come. We debated numerous questions:

- Can we afford this?
- Is this the right location?
- Does this building give us long-term growth potential?
- Will people move with us?
- Will they give to support it?
- Will we sink the entire thing if something goes wrong?
- Is this what God is calling us to?
- How do we know for sure?

Once we announced our decision to the congregation and enthusiasm for the future began to build, I remained tied up in decision after decision, each one more complicated than the one before. Every decision carried long-term implications, and often I felt horribly inadequate to make those decisions.

In what should have been one of the most exciting seasons of my career and one of my biggest accomplishments as a leader, I found my stomach tied up in knots and my head routinely about to explode. It was absolutely overwhelming.

Can you relate?

I bet there is a decision that you've faced that feels just a bit bigger than you're qualified to handle. Congratulations! I believe that's a sign that you are leading well. Leaders are decision makers. That's what sets you apart and makes your leadership necessary.

Most people aren't good at making decisions, especially not the ones that affect someone other than themselves. If everyone could make the decisions, the big decisions, the tough ones, they probably wouldn't need a leader so desperately. As Emperor Napoleon Bonaparte once said, "Nothing is more difficult, and therefore more precious, than to be able to decide."[1]

You are needed for the leadership that you bring, especially in decision making. Good decision making isn't tied to gender, of course. But I tend to believe we women might have an edge when it comes to decision making because of that thing called intuition. We may also have an extra curse: that ugly monster called insecurity. Since we tackled insecurity in chapter 4, let's focus on intuition and its ability to help us make confident decisions.

YOUR HEART MATTERS

Good decision making is an overflow of a heart that is in tune with God. As a leader who is a follower of Christ, you are going to be most confident in your decisions when you are confident in who you are in Christ and confident that he has placed you in your position of leadership at this time for this purpose. You are not there by accident. God works "all things together for good" (Romans 8:28). If you believe that, you have to trust that he will equip you for what he's called you to do.

The irony is that as much as we believe that God has called us to our roles and responsibilities, we easily find ourselves distracted by doubt and fear. At the slightest concern or question mark, especially in our decisions, we begin to believe that we can't do this. That kind of thinking is not true, correct, or helpful.

The starting point for your confidence in decision making has to come from believing that you are where God has called you to be. When you find yourself questioning this, you have to go back to those moments where you knew beyond a shadow of a doubt that God was leading you.

"FOR SUCH A TIME AS THIS"

You know the story well. We women leaders tend to cling to Esther as an inspiring woman from scripture. But reread Esther through a new lens. Notice how she wasn't so confident in what she needed to do. She questioned Mordecai's instruction to go to the king because she could be put to death if she did that. As she processed the decision she needed to make, she asked for all the Jewish people to join her in three days of prayer and fasting. Listen to her confidence in this next step: "Then Esther sent this reply to Mordecai: 'Go, gather together all the Jews who are in Susa, and fast for me. Do not eat or drink for three days, night or day. I and my maids will fast as you do. When this is done, I will go to the king, even though it is against the law. And if I perish, I perish'" (Esther 4:15–16).

Have you experienced a "for such a time as this" moment—a situation where in hindsight, you can see exactly why God led you there and directed your steps even though you couldn't see the outcome clearly?

You have to find a way to mark those moments so that you remember them on the days when what God is calling you to doesn't feel very secure.

REMAIN IN HIM

You also have to remain connected. Jesus said, "I am the vine; you are the branches. If you remain in me and I in you, you will bear much fruit; apart from me you can do nothing" (John 15:5). You surely know this verse well, but let the words sink in for a minute: "Apart from me [God] you can do nothing." Great leadership and good decision making are an overflow of a heart that is well connected. We can't lead from a place of emptiness, and we certainly can't make good decisions when we are running on spiritual fumes.

INSTINCTS, GUT, INTUITION, DISCERNMENT, AND HOLY SPIRIT

As you approach decision making as a leader, you have to trust your gut. *Instincts, intuition, discernment, the Holy Spirit:* for this conversation, I'm using those words interchangeably because I'm assuming that your instincts, gut, or intuition as a Christ follower are the things that the Holy Spirit is telling you through the spiritual gift of discernment.

As a leader, more specifically a steward of the people and resources God has entrusted you to lead, you need discernment to make the decisions that you face daily. This confidence in discernment is what combats the indecision you may find yourself facing.

FAITH WITHOUT DETAILS

Trying to make a large decision too soon often paralyzes my decision making. As a very self-aware control freak, I can identify this tendency in myself pretty quickly. From the beginning, I want to know the end. I want to figure out the entire challenge before I even begin. I want a clear-cut path before I enter the forest. The reality is that that's not reality. Most decisions we face as leaders are step-by-step decisions. In fact, I don't believe that God wants us always to know how things finish; it removes our need for trust and faith in him. I once heard Pastor Craig Groeschel say, "God loves you enough not to give you all the details." If we knew all the details, we might just give up before we even started.

But God does tell us how things end: "'For I know the plans I have for you,' declares the Lord, 'plans to prosper you and not to harm you, plans to give you hope and a future'" (Jeremiah 29:11). We're not always satisfied with that because it's vague—hopeful, yes, but vague. He tells us he has it under control but doesn't give us all the details. The details would probably be too much for us. I'm guessing you have had one of those seasons of life where after you came through it, you look back and marvel at all that God led you through. If you had known what the journey looked like ahead of time, there's a good chance you wouldn't have started it.

My friend Shannon is a strong and powerful leader who is president of a successful marketing company while also juggling the responsibilities of a committed wife, dedicated mom to two lovely daughters, and plenty of volunteering with her church. While her life seemingly didn't have room for more, Shannon and her husband really sensed God leading them to adopt a child from Ethiopia. I happened to be in a meeting with Shannon the day that she was sent a picture of the precious little boy whom they would be adopting. The tears of joy abounded in that room as we celebrated with her.

As their family continued the process for adoption, the agency surprisingly reached out to them to ask them to consider adopting a second little boy from the same orphanage. A little overwhelmed but certain that this was God's direction, they agreed, and within six months, they brought both boys home to complete their family of six.

Their first Christmas as a new family was incredibly joyful. The boys were settling into routine and were all adjusting to their new dynamics when the New Year brought a surprise: Shannon was pregnant. For a woman who planned to have only two children, this was simply overwhelming. She questioned God and questioned their ability to handle it all. Had God shown her this part of her story previous to their decision to adopt, she admits they may have never stepped out into the place of obedience and faith.

NEXT-BEST-STEP DECISIONS

Most of our decisions in life and leadership will be "next-best-step" decisions. What is the next best step that God is asking you to take or to lead your team through? Taking the next best step is where faith and obedience collide: faith for the unknown and obedience to the next step of action.

Let's go back to Esther's story.

Scripture doesn't really explain why, but notice that even when Esther approached King Xerxes, she doesn't immediately share her request even though he extended his scepter to her to spare her life. Instead she asked for a banquet with him by which to share her request. And then still at that banquet, she asks for another banquet. Why did she delay her request multiple times when she found favor with the king in her first encounter with him? I can only assume that she must have been responding to the discernment of the situation and being obedient to the next best step. We know that ultimately, the delay of that conversation allowed Haman's evil plot to be exposed and Mordecai to be honored, making way for the king to eagerly grant her request.

When Esther made a decision, it was always a next-step decision. Every decision faced numerous outcomes that were beyond her control. Knowing she couldn't control the outcomes, she simply remained faithful to her next step.

In my experience, God doesn't give us the entire route all at one time. He gives us next steps, step-by-step, day-by-day. Learning to be comfortable and confident in those steps of obedience is what marks you as a great leader.

WHY YOU CAN'T DECIDE

Although we know in our hearts that we need to discern God's leading in our decision making, we still find ourselves paralyzed by indecision more often than we like to admit. Why? I believe it's because indecision taps into some of the issues we perpetually wrestle with:

- Control
- Impatience
- Listening
- Avoidance
- Fatigue

Control

We wrestle with indecision because of our need to control. Decision making is terrifying because if we get it wrong, we fear losing control. Part of what we have to come to grips with in decision making is that for as much as we can make calculated and carefully controlled decisions, we are absolutely powerless to control the outcomes. Though it's frustrating, we have to get to a place where we are confident and secure in the decisions that we make, be prepared to give an account for why we made them, and then trust the outcomes to God.

Impatience

Sometimes good decisions require waiting. We might be waiting on God for clarity, direction, or permission to move. We might be waiting on others who are part of the decision-making process. Whatever is causing our wait often seems unbearable. Imagine Esther's impatience as she waited for the right timing to ask the king to spare her people. Our anxious hearts must learn to wait patiently sometimes.

Listening

Sometimes we're unable to make decisions because we're not willing to stop and listen. In a world where distractions are endless, listening becomes more and more difficult. I sometimes find myself dodging the quiet. I don't know what I'm afraid of there. Perhaps I'm more afraid of what I'll miss than what I'll hear. I'm afraid of missing the latest announcement on Twitter or the recent office gossip. But my inability to shut out the noise keeps me distracted from really listening for God's voice of discernment and direction.

Avoidance

I recently came home from a particularly long and stressful day at work. All it took was a well-intended, "How was your day?"

inquiry from my husband to trigger an emotional explosion that I instantly regretted. I didn't even realize it was coming. A decision I was facing was wearing on me much more than I realized, and as I let go of all I was holding in, I startled myself and probably my husband (although he played it very cool). I let go of some of the leadership fears I was stuffing inside, and given the force with which they came out, I'd apparently been stuffing for a while!

That little explosion was a reminder to me that leaders and their decisions aren't always popular. That's really what I was upset about. I needed to make a decision that wasn't necessarily popular, but I knew in my heart it was right and it was the best thing for our organization at the time.

Leaders lead people to accomplish things that they are generally afraid of doing on their own. They call us to greatness, but often that's accompanied by perseverance and trial. Great leaders are okay with making people uncomfortable because they see the payoff that the average person cannot discern.

Sometimes it's not as much that we can't decide but that we don't want to decide. We don't want to make the unpopular decisions. We're afraid of what others may perceive of us. We're afraid of being labeled with the "b" word (you know what it rhymes with).

Fatigue

Sometimes we're just too tired to decide.

It was a simple decision, but I just couldn't make it. My assistant was picking up lunch for me because I had a string of back-to-back meetings in an already hectic week. A few minutes after she left, I got a call from her that the restaurant was out of what I had ordered. It seems simple enough looking back to think that I could have just ordered something else, but I couldn't. I didn't know what else I wanted. In fact I was more willing to go without lunch than to have to make another decision.

I went home that night thinking, *What in the world is wrong with me? I can't even make a simple decision about lunch!*

It turns out that there is a name for this condition: *decision fatigue*. A recent article in the *New York Times* explained it this way:

> Decision fatigue helps explain why ordinarily sensible people get angry at colleagues and families, splurge on clothes, buy junk food at the supermarket and can't resist the dealer's offer to rustproof their new car. No matter how rational and high-minded you try to be, you can't make decision after decision without paying a biological price. It's different from ordinary physical fatigue—you're not consciously aware of being tired—but you're low on mental energy. The more choices you make throughout the day, the harder each one becomes for your brain, and eventually it looks for shortcuts, usually in either of two different ways. One shortcut is to become reckless: to act impulsively instead of expending the energy to first think through the consequences. (Sure, tweet that photo! What could go wrong?) The other shortcut is the ultimate energy saver: do nothing. Instead of agonizing over decisions, avoid any choice. Ducking a decision often creates bigger problems in the long run, but for the moment, it eases the mental strain.[2]

Sound familiar?

This is a challenge to our leadership that we need to be hyperaware of. Dangerous, erratic behavior can result from simply being too tired to decide.

From a spiritual perspective I think decision fatigue can be a result of relying too much on our own strength. In our drive and determination as leaders, we can fall victim to the mentality of "if it's meant to be it's up to me."[3] I am constantly challenged by the scripture: "Trust in the Lord with all your heart and lean not on your own understanding; in all your ways submit to him, and he will make your paths straight" (Proverbs 3:5–6). When we rely too much on our own understanding, we lose God's guidance in our lives.

I also believe that decision fatigue is a by-product of not observing the spiritual discipline of Sabbath. I'll admit that I'm enormously guilty of this. I just can't resist that phone call I need to make or that quick stop by the office or one more e-mail that can't wait until Monday. When I resist God's command of Sabbath, I'm doubting God's sovereignty and faithfulness in my life.

SOLUTIONS FOR INDECISION

I wish that I could tell you that there was a magical moment where all of a sudden I became a great decision maker. In fact, the older I get and the more I learn, the more I realize how much I don't know. And at the same time that I'm realizing how much I really don't know, the more leadership decisions I find myself facing! But there are a few things that I do to help me embrace my role as a leader who needs to make confident decisions.

Accept Responsibility

As a leader, it's your responsibility to make decisions. That's why you're the leader. If everyone else knew what to do, they wouldn't need you to lead them. Sometimes I have to remind myself of this. It doesn't necessarily erase the fear, doubt, or uncertainty that I may be facing, but it's the way that I remind myself that God has put me in a position of leadership for a reason and I must take responsibility for that.

Follow a Formula

A few simple steps can help you start making progress in decision making:

Step 1: Identify the problem or issue.
Step 2: Investigate it. Study it. Understand it.
Step 3: Seek input from those most closely associated with it
Step 4: Pray seriously. Don't pray flippant, on-the-fly prayers. Carve out some time with God to seek discernment.

Step 5: Make the decision expeditiously. Once you've discerned
   God's direction, don't delay.

Esther's story is a great example of this formula at work. When
Esther learned of the king's decree to kill all the Jews (step 1),
she sent one of her servants to get the details from Mordecai
(Esther 4:4–6) (step 2). In verses 9 to 14, she seeks additional
counsel from Mordecai about the ramifications of going to the
king without being summoned (step 3), and then, in verses 15
to 17, she asks Mordecai to gather all the Jews to pray and fast
together (step 4). In chapter 5 she moves forward with her decision
to approach the king (step 5).

While our decision may not be a life-or-death situation as
Esther's was, many of the decisions we face become easier when
we break them down and take them step-by-step.

How quickly you move through this formula may vary from
decision to decision. Some decisions may be quick; others may
take a good deal of time. The spirit of the process is the key.
Spend time seeking to understand the issue from all angles, pray
for discernment, and act on your instincts. If your instincts tell you
to slow down, do that; if your instincts tell you to move forward
with your decision, don't delay.

Trust God

Founder of A21 and dynamic speaker Christine Caine had some
useful thoughts on trusting God in decision making, particularly
the questions she asks at what she calls the crossroads of decision
making:

- Why would I?
- Why won't I?
- Why don't I?
- Why shouldn't I?
- Why should I?
- Why aren't I?

- What regret will I have if I don't?
- What might happen if I do?
- What will I never know if I don't?
- What will it cost if I do?
- What will it cost if I don't?

She continues,

There are many more questions, but I think you get the point. After you have asked the questions, analyzed your answers, revisited your questions, concerns, and analysis a dozen times, and you still come up with the same nagging internal sense that you need to take the next step, then all I can say is: start running towards that cliff's edge and take the leap of faith!

You will find that God is waiting for you to jump and He will give you wings to fly. The next step is often on the other side of a quantum leap into the unknown.

It's called trusting God.[4]

As leaders, we're counted on to make good decisions but the good news is that we're not intended to make those decisions alone! Ideally you have a good support network around you for counsel and guidance (see chapter 5 for more suggestions), and most important, God is interested in guiding our decisions. Fight against the voice of pride that tries to convince you that you have to have it all figured out. Battle the doubts and insecurities that try to convince you not to act. Those are simply arguments of the enemy that serve to derail you and keep you off focus as a leader. You have been called and equipped for such a time as this to guide, lead, and decide.

QUESTIONS FOR REFLECTION AND DISCUSSION

1. Where in your life is indecision holding you back?
2. Describe a time when you sensed God's direction in making a decision.

3. Identify a situation in which you need to be taking the next best step.

4. What issue most commonly traps you with indecision: control, impatience, listening, avoidance, or fatigue? What are some of the ways you can avoid this trap?

CHAPTER
7

GO BIG OR GO HOME

The walls were blue. I (Sherry) remember because I had been staring at them for what seemed like hours. I was inside the teachers' lounge bathroom, and I wasn't planning on coming out any time soon. I was the assistant principal at a struggling inner-city elementary school, and I had just received the results of our state testing: they weren't good.

Our school was feeling the pressure, just as all the others in the district were, to bring up our scores in reading and math. But we all wanted our kids also to embrace a love for reading and see the important part mathematics played in their everyday world. I so wanted our students, MY students, to do well. I knew they were working hard, I knew we had a winning strategy, and I believed in them—so much so that I had thrown down the challenge that we could raise our math scores by a whopping 20 percent over the previous year, ignoring the fact that we had never made an increase even half that big.

Why in the world had I set a goal so audacious? And why in the world had I said it out loud? It was a tough moment for me. I remember thinking a very childish thought sitting in that bathroom: *Dreaming big is stupid. It's just setting yourself up for disappointment.*

TINY HEART SYNDROME

It was with that thought that I opened the door to what I call *tiny heart syndrome*. Every leader wants to dream big, but we've all seen big dreams that didn't pan out. We've watched while other leaders let themselves bust outside the walls of the proverbial box, only to have the lid slam in their face. We've all felt just a little sorry for those leaders, and maybe some of us have made the mental note: *don't dream too big or you'll wind up embarrassing yourself, just like them.*

Even as I write this, my leadership role has changed in a big way. For the first time in my life, I find myself the CEO of a large, international organization: Mothers of Preschoolers International (MOPS). Coming into this role, I felt strongly that God was prompting me to dream big. My organization currently reaches over 100,000 moms in thirty-two countries through mom-connection groups with discussions and activities that introduce them to Christ and expose them to life-changing leadership development opportunities. But isn't the pool of moms and potential leaders much greater than 100,000? I have felt God's whisper, "Dream big with me, and let me show you what I can do." But then my thoughts go back to the blue bathroom and my failure, which happened over fifteen years ago. And this is what is so debilitating, devastatingly limiting about tiny heart syndrome. In my case, it prompted memories that tried to limit me to think small out of fear instead of dreaming big out of faith, hand in hand with God, who can make it happen. It's temptingly safe and deceptively comfortable.

THINKING A LITTLE BIT CRAZY

Let me juxtapose these tales of my experience with a story of a woman I met while doing some research for Leadership Network. Over the course of a year, I interviewed 120 women about their experience in leadership, asking them to share their biggest successes as well as their deepest challenges. One woman's story will forever stand out to me, not because of her remarkable success, but because of her indomitable ability to dream.

She was a stay-at-home mom, and it all started with a personal need. She needed to go back to work for extra income now that her kids were older, but she wasn't sure what to do. One of her passions was walking dogs. She knew she could start a dog walking business, but something inside her pulled her heart to something bigger. One morning she happened to read a newspaper article about women from Third World countries being brought to her city and forced into the sex trade industry. Now she not only felt a pull but a huge stir in her heart. What could she do about this? The thought kept running in her head: *Just go back to what you know. You know dogs. Just stick with that.* It was the tiny heart syndrome rearing its ugly head, but she didn't listen. She couldn't stop thinking about these women, some of them no older than her children. She knew a dream was being born in her heart, but it was bigger than what she could outline on her own.

She formed what she called a dream team of like-minded women; she knew they would listen to her ramblings and cheer her on. Week after week they met as she shared what was on her heart. Could she somehow start a dog walking business that could fund a ministry to the women caught in sex trafficking and provide them with a safe place to go? This was a group that knew how to dream big, and they encouraged her to do the same. As the dream took shape, she formed another group, the Down and Dirty Club, comprising businesspeople, both men and women, who could talk about revenue streams, business plans, and financial strategy.

After months of dreaming and planning, her dream began to become a reality. She started a gourmet dog food business, which appealed to upper-income dog owners in her community, paired with a dog walking business that spotlighted the dogs in superhero costumes on their daily walks. She said she was often stopped and asked about the costumes, and she would reply that the proceeds from the gourmet food these dogs were eating were rescuing women caught in sex trafficking. The funds were being used to set up counseling and job opportunities for the women, and the dogs were indeed heroes. The response was phenomenal. Everyone wanted their dogs to be superheroes too, and her business exploded. She talked with her church and gained its partnership in forming the ministry to the women and began to talk to city officials to gain political support. My most recent conversation with this woman was filled with talk of building a safe house and creating a program to provide these women with business training in microfinance.

It all had started as a crazy thought over a cup of coffee at her kitchen table and a refusal to ignore the tug in her heart. When I asked her if she had gotten pushback on her dream, she laughed. She said everyone told her she was crazy, and she thought so herself many times. But the thought of walking away from the opportunity to do something this big was unthinkable. She also knew she didn't know what she was doing, but she knew the God who did. What a great example of overcoming tiny heart syndrome.

LESSONS FROM NEHEMIAH

Part of dreaming big as a leader means exposing your vulnerabilities and putting yourself out there for people to tell you all the reasons you can't. And there will be many. But dreaming big with God means holding his hand, walking in faith that he *is* there, and stubbornly staring down the opposition.

One of my favorite stories from the Bible is about Nehemiah. Not only was he a world-class leader, but he was a big dreamer as well. His beloved city, Jerusalem, had fallen to ruin. The walls had been destroyed, the gates that protected the city broken, the hope of his beloved people at an all-time low. The city lay exposed and vulnerable to its enemies. When Nehemiah learned of this, it literally broke his heart, and he cried out to God in distress. God answered, "I can fix that," and together they went after it.

Nehemiah was a man who saw the problem and didn't shrink back from going after it with all he had. And he knew where to go for help. I've read this story many times not only because of its leadership principles, but because it's a reminder of what dreaming big with God can accomplish. Here are some lessons I've learned from Nehemiah.

Nehemiah Didn't Step Ahead of God

When Nehemiah heard about the condition of his beloved brothers and sisters in Jerusalem and the condition of the city walls, he wasn't just upset; he stepped into holy discontent. His sources told him of the disorganization and the terrible morale, and he reached the point where he couldn't bear to hear any more. This part of the story always reminds me of the movie *Popeye*, when, in response to being bullied by his archenemy Bluto, Popeye says, "I've had all I can stands and I just can't stands no more." Exactly. Having a stirring in your heart that won't let you walk away or sit idle is a crucial part of dreaming big. Nehemiah felt this and spent the next several days in fasting, prayer, and, most important, humble repentance. Before he asked for God's help, he asked for God's forgiveness for his own pride and arrogance and that of his people that had gotten them into this situation in the first place. This allowed God to remove any issues of the heart that might get in the way.

A critical lesson, and one I remind myself of often, is this: don't step ahead of God and what he needs to work in *you* first. This is where I think I've gotten off track in the past. I've pursued Sherry dreams, which were good things but not necessarily God dreams. Had I started with an attitude of humility and repentance when I boldly spoke my ambitious dream for my students in Houston? I don't think so. Had I poured out my heart to God and listened for his direction before I started my plan? Of course, my students' performing to their utmost ability was a good thing, but had I let it be a God thing instead of a Sherry thing? Going back to my thought in the bathroom, I realized that dreaming big isn't stupid, but dreaming big without God is foolish.

But how many times as leaders do we do just that? We have an idea, a big dream, that is so awesome that we think, *How can it not be a God dream?* We plan, we strategize, we start our implementation, and then we invite God in and wonder why he doesn't bless us. Could it be that we stepped out in front of God without hearing from him first?

Nehemiah Quietly Did His Homework

Nehemiah didn't just sit idle and let God do all the work. He researched what he would need to attack the huge dream of rebuilding Jerusalem. The Bible tells us he gathered his resources and supplies and went through the proper channels for approval. He humbly approached the king and asked for a letter of recommendation, knowing this would gain him favor and pave the way. The Bible also tells us he kept his mouth shut during the research phase. Nehemiah says, "After I had been there three days, I got up in the middle of the night, I and a few men who were with me. I hadn't told anyone what my God had put in my heart to do for Jerusalem" (Nehemiah 2:11–12). Nehemiah wisely stayed quiet until he had gathered the facts. When it came time to make his dream known, he knew what he was up against and had the plan to address it.

What great guidelines to remember as leaders:

- Do your due diligence in the form of research and gathering.
- Slow down and hear from God.
- Don't speak your plan too quickly; give God the time to work in the hearts of those around you.
- Make sure that when you share your plan, it's not about broadcasting the win for you, but what God can do.

Nehemiah Didn't Try to Be a Lone Ranger

Nehemiah never tried to do it alone. He enlisted the help of all the stakeholders: the Jewish people, the priests, nobles, and local officials. Chapter 2 (verses 17 and 18) lets us in on a key fact: Nehemiah didn't try to sugarcoat the dream to those who would help him pull it off. Nehemiah said, "Then I gave them my report: 'Face it: we're in a bad way here. Jerusalem is a wreck; its gates are burned up. Come—let's build the wall of Jerusalem and not live with this disgrace any longer.' I told them how God was supporting me and how the king was backing me up. They said, 'We're with you. Let's get started.' They rolled up their sleeves, ready for the good work."

Part of enlisting your team is being honest about what's ahead. You can't do it alone, and you shouldn't even try. But enlisting help doesn't mean hiding the commitment and sacrifice that will be required in getting from here to there just to rally the enthusiasm or get their help. Be honest about the situation, include the vision for where you are going, and let the others know you're following God every step of the way.

Nehemiah Refused to Quit

Nehemiah met big resistance from Sanballat and Tobias, two prominent leaders of the day. They were respected, commanded attention, and weren't pleased that Nehemiah had stepped in with a new vision. According to Nehemiah 2:19, "When Sanballat the Horonite, Tobiah the Ammonite official, and Geshem the Arab heard about it, they laughed at us, mocking, 'Ha! What do you think you're doing? Do you think you can cross the king?'" I love Nehemiah's bold response in chapter 2:20: "The God-of-Heaven will make sure we succeed. We're his servants and we're going to work, rebuilding. You can keep your nose out of it. You get no say in this—Jerusalem's none of your business!"

Don't you love leadership confidence when it's grounded in the undeniable presence and power of God? Sometimes it's a thin line between holy confidence and selfish stubbornness, but this is where the time invested in seeking and listening to God comes in. If God is leading you, you don't have to buckle when resistance hits. You can afford to stand firm because you don't stand alone. Here's another lesson I've learned from Nehemiah: just because you tell those against you to back off, it doesn't mean they'll listen. Read on in Nehemiah 4: 7–9: "When Sanballat, Tobiah, the Arabs, the Ammonites, and the Ashdodites heard that the repairs of the walls of Jerusalem were going so well—that the breaks in the wall were being fixed—they were absolutely furious. They put their heads together and decided to fight against Jerusalem and create as much trouble as they could. We countered with prayer to our God and set a round-the-clock guard against them."

It's always tempting to throw up our hands when faced with backbiting, gossip, and others rallying against us. This is where I let Nehemiah inspire me with his no-fail method: he led his team in going straight to God, and instead of giving up, they stepped up their efforts with twenty-four-hour surveillance. It was a godly form of looking his opposition right in the eye and saying, "Take that!"

LESSONS FROM A NAPKIN

In my Bible I keep a small napkin that has frayed edges and a few stains. I keep it there to remind me of a dark day in my leadership as children's ministry pastor when I had laid out a plan that I thought was well conceived and much needed. My team had not objected to the plan, but had quietly walked away and then invested in some destructive gossip and backbiting. I was hurt, but I had to admit I hadn't handled everything well in the process. As I read the story of Nehemiah again in one of my favorite coffee places, I wrote these key lessons on my napkin, with the title "Nehemiah" at the top:

- Wait for God.
- Do your homework.
- Don't do it alone.
- Never give up.

That napkin has served me well. When I hit moments when discouragement threatens to overwhelm, I pull out my napkin and remember Nehemiah. He faced setbacks and opposition at every turn, but we don't see him running for the school bathroom to hide. He gathered his wits, his team, and his resources and made sure he was following God at every turn. That napkin reminds me I can do the same. So can you.

Debbie's Story

I met Debbie Eaton during my recent time in California. She serves as the women's ministry director at Saddleback Church in Lake Forest. The first thing I noticed about Debbie was the bigness of her hug. The first time we were introduced, she threw her arms around me and drew me in. As she talked, the joy poured out of her voice. Her dream for women becoming everything that God designed them to be was as big as her hug, and I liked her from the start. She shared with me that her women's ministry had gone through a recent change when the economic crisis hit California, and she was forced to move from a staffed women's ministry that served thousands of women in small groups, Bible studies, and various ministry opportunities to a ministry completely driven by volunteers. At first it was overwhelming. How would she continue to serve all these women when it felt as if she was going to have to do it all by herself? But the bigness of the task didn't stop Debbie from achieving her dream of helping women grow in their relationship with God, in fact it just got bigger. I invited Debbie to share her story here.

❖

I love dreaming big, and it was so easy when I had a staff of eight part-time women. We enjoyed dreaming together and being part of a thriving ministry that served women in so many ways. The team was passionate, loyal, and accountable, and we had so much fun together. Ministry was good. Then the wind was taken out of me: I was told that the paid part-time staff would need to become all volunteer. To say that I was angry, discouraged, and confused is an understatement. As you might imagine, there was a slow attrition as those eight bowed out for other employment or opportunities. Please do not think less of these women. It was an opportunity for them to revisit a place to serve, and most had needed the income. I remember crying out to God, saying, "I thought you gave me a dream to build women into all they could be with a dream team. I can't do this alone."

I was frustrated, scared, and, frankly, ready to give up. I remember the day I sat with a dear friend, complaining, when she took me to a passage in 2 Chronicles 20:17: "You will not need to fight this battle. Take up your positions; stand firm and see the deliverance the Lord will give you. Do not be afraid; do not be discouraged. Go out to face them tomorrow and the Lord will be with you." I was at a crossroad and had to make a choice: Would I pout, quit, and give up, or trust God that if he placed this dream in the depth of my heart and soul, surely he would provide all that was necessary to birth and nurture the dream?

I put my trust in God and made an important decision at that time that has resulted in building a volunteer team that is stronger, healthier, and far more rewarding than a paid staff.

My decision that day was that no woman would be an interruption. If God meant me to build a volunteer team, then he would place the women in my path. That meant that at Starbucks, Target, the grocery store, the airport, the gym, ball fields, I would stop, listen, and engage with women who needed to hear that they had something worthwhile to invest in other women, and I would invite them to join the women's ministry team. This was hard because I had no funds to pay them and had no idea how much a volunteer would be willing to take on, but I found that there were so many women who had attended our church for years and had been looking for an opportunity to serve, but no one had opened the door with a personal invitation. I stepped out in faith and asked them, and within a few months, I had an army of ordinary women volunteers who are inspired to serve in extraordinary ways and with no expectation of a paycheck.

Leading a healthy volunteer ministry requires a team that knows they are critical to the dream, are inspired to share the dream, invite others to be part of the dream, and celebrate the success of the dream. I have learned and experienced that God will always provide the people, resources, and strength needed to live out the dream he has placed in your soul. Remember it is God's dream that we have the honor to live out. Be genuine and authentic, speak words of encouragement, and give big hugs.

FOR EVERY LEADER

As Debbie's story so beautifully illustrates, every obstacle to our dreams brings with it the choice to let that obstacle become a roadblock that leads to giving up or to letting God engineer a detour. Not giving up is hard and often downright scary. But here's what I'm learning: if you lead in any capacity, God is calling you to dream big. In my position as CEO of MOPS, I'm responsible to my organization and to those I lead to take Nehemiah's lessons to heart. I can't afford to step out ahead of God. My team is counting on me to come before God with authentic humility and seek his dreams, not mine. It's crucial that I do my homework and wait for God's timing. I can't do it alone, and I have to have the courage not to quit, even when quitting would be a relief. I love Winston Churchill's challenge to the boys at Harrow School in 1941 when he admonished them to stay true to their dreams. His closing words were, "Never, never, in nothing great or small, large or petty, never give in except to convictions of honour and good sense. Never yield to force; never yield to the apparently overwhelming might of the enemy."[1]

As a leader, I'm going for blue sky dreaming hand-in-hand with God, the author of big dreams, and I hope you'll join me. I pray that God will challenge your heart with big dreams that may seem impossible, that cause you to run to him, and that when you do, he'll fill you with the courage to never give up.

QUESTIONS FOR REFLECTION AND DISCUSSION

1. When in your leadership do you notice tiny heart syndrome?
2. What scares you most about dreaming big?
3. Do you work in an environment that encourages big thinking? If not, are there things you can do to change this? What are they?

CHAPTER 8

LEADING MEN

As a leader at a large church, I (Sherry) was optimistic, enthusiastic, and unknowingly naive. The norm in the secular elementary education I had been part of was that a male teacher would have a female supervisor and work on a team of mostly women. It was something expected and usual. So picture enthusiastic me, stepping into leading a mixed-gender team, taking the place of a male pastor who had led the team for several years. No big deal, right?

It started with the opportunity to lead a young man in his first ministry position. He had had previous experience with a woman supervisor that had not gone well, so our relationship began with suspicious distrust. I would find myself thinking, *Why isn't he open about his team schedule and his ideas? Why does he seem defensive when I ask questions about his projects? Why is he so quiet in our team meetings?* Instead of asking him these questions directly, I pressed for details about what he was doing, which put him even more on the defensive. I would question, he would grow ever more silent, and we both felt that we were working in opposite directions.

Soon I started to notice tension between his wife and me as well. When we encountered each other at church, what used to be an easy, casual conversation was now tension filled and strained.

I was perplexed. What did my working relationship with him have to do with her? A more seasoned leader would have been able to answer that straight away: he felt I didn't trust him or respect his abilities, and this made her defensive about her husband. He felt micromanaged and dishonored. This made her angry and resentful of me, which added fuel to his fire. Now I had not one unhappy team member but an anxious, unhappy wife as well.

Even as I write this today, this experience, which happened over fifteen years ago, still makes my stomach hurt. My mind goes back to how confused and desperate I felt. We were both intelligent people who were passionate about ministry, and we both loved the Lord with all our hearts. So why couldn't we work together without this tension?

Looking at the situation through his eyes, I now have more understanding. His previous supervisor had had a dictatorial manner. She insisted on numerous detailed reports and became irate when they weren't delivered. Their team meetings were often emotion filled and unpredictable, often leaving this young leader to wonder what explosion was coming next. Up to the time I started working with him, this had been his only encounter with a woman supervisor. It also happened to mirror some of the experiences he had had with his sisters and mom. Pile onto this the fact that I was inexperienced and clueless as to what this young leader needed from me. It was a recipe for disaster.

There isn't a leader reading this book who doesn't want to succeed when it comes to working together with the opposite sex. But I think we can all agree that sometimes it's complicated, frustrating, and just plain hard. Men and women have different communication styles and react with different levels of emotion. Then, just for fun, let's throw in fear of sexual tension and deeply rooted theological differences. In fact, it's amazing that any mixed-gender teams get anything accomplished.

Let's dig a little deeper into some of these areas of potential conflict.

WE AREN'T SPEAKING THE SAME LANGUAGE

I watched with interest the other day as a woman on my staff shared an idea with my team. She talked animatedly, using her hands often. Her cadence was fast, and her face mirrored her excitement. She unpacked each part of the idea, giving the background, the history of how the idea had come to her in the middle of the night, and then she relayed every word of the conversation she had had with her husband the next morning as she shared the idea with him, even mentioning the new breakfast burrito she had eaten.

I also watched with interest as the guy sitting next to me began to sink down into his chair lower and lower until he looked like a TV ad for cheap recliners. I'm not positive, but from his sighing and the way he held up his head with a sagging arm, I also suspect his eyes may have rolled back in his head once or twice. What was going on was that this woman was literally talking the poor fellow to death. Her idea was good, but she was using too many words to tell it. He had actually liked the idea and after the first couple of sentences had tried to interrupt her to ask a question, but she bulldozed on. He was drowning in details.

I've found myself in such an assault with the guys on my team, and unfortunately, I was the assaulter. Many of them needed just the straightforward facts, and I piled on the details, the background, the emotion, and everything but the kitchen sink. In the reverse, I've sometimes been bothered when a guy on my team has seemed to yadda-yadda through an idea or situation, giving the briefest of details and then moving on. *Wait*, I think. *What happened after that? How did you feel about it? And then what did you say?* These were all questions I wanted to ask, but he didn't seem to want to share this information. The reason? It's pretty simple: men and women speak and receive information differently, and as leaders, we have to be sensitive to this. Do the men on your team get impatient when you unpack too much? Are you using too many words when just a few will do? Not paying attention to this will sometimes cause them to shut down and seem distant.

THERE'S NO CRYING IN BASEBALL

I have a favorite scene from the Tom Hanks movie *A League of Their Own* that epitomizes the difference that exists in how women and men react emotionally. Hanks's character is in way over his head in coaching an all-women's baseball team and finds himself having to correct his right fielder after she made a stupid mistake. He begins with his customary name-calling and yelling, and she responds by bursting in tears. A look of disbelief comes over his face. He shoots a stream of tobacco juice out of his mouth, and says, "Are you crying?! There's no crying in baseball!"

This is exactly how many men feel about emotional outbursts in the workplace. I spoke the other day with a man on my team who relayed a story about a team retreat he had attended with a woman leader. When I asked how it went, he used the word *miserable*. He said all the women in the room had cried, some more than once, and he had never wanted so badly to just go home. The woman leader encouraged everyone to bare their feelings and share honestly about a recent tension they had all gone through. He said it made his skin itch. He was there to follow the agenda, which to him indicated they were going to analyze their return on investment from the previous semester, outline the team goals for the next year, and formulate their strategy. He was there to get stuff done. Instead there was crying.

Let me take a minute to address tears and pouting. God made women with tender hearts and sensitive natures. This is a good thing. However, this doesn't mean we have the right to bring meetings to a halt because we erupt into tears when someone disagrees or challenges us or even embarrasses us in public. The worst thing—let me repeat *the worst thing*—you can do as a women leader is to let your emotions control you. It puts men at a disadvantage because they don't always know how to react. It causes them to wonder, *Should I just ignore it? Should we stop everything and address it? Should I jump up and get her a tissue?* Neither is it okay to clam up and shut down, sending the clear message with your silence, *I'm not okay.* For some of the men on our team, it causes them to unconsciously acknowledge, *Yep, here we go. This is what it's like to work with women.*

Even when this is the opposite of your intention, it can make you look manipulative and overly sensitive and can cause you to lose credibility. Will there be appropriate times when emotion will overcome you? Absolutely. When God has just moved in a big way and answered miraculously, or when a family in your church is suffering and sharing the story makes your eyes well up, it's perfectly appropriate to acknowledge this, join together as a team, and have a moment. There may be times when someone on your team is experiencing personal pain, and sometimes that person will be you. It's okay during these times to show your human side and be vulnerable. It's *not* okay to shut down a discussion or disagreement with an outburst of tears because your feelings are hurt or you're not getting your way.

I have a brilliant, articulate friend who cries easily. She hates this about herself and has tried everything to stop it. When she gets frustrated or is in a heated discussion, she sometimes loses the ability to speak clearly, her face turns red and blotchy, and the tears start to roll. Yet she works in a high-pressure organization where she leads a team of mostly men. When I asked her how she handles this, she said she's learned to roll with it. When she feels her throat begin to tighten and the tears well up, she stops and announces, "I need a ten-minute water break." Note that she's using the word *water* here in a figurative way: she means she needs to step outside and let her eyes leak and get control of herself. Brilliant!

She said the guys on her team have told her they appreciate this and have learned to do it themselves when they have felt their tempers flair. They all had a good laugh one day when one of the guys announced during a tension-filled budget meeting, "I need ten minutes to step outside and punch someone in the head."

The bottom line here is that emotion is going to threaten to overwhelm all of us, men and women, from time to time. The important thing as a leader is how you choose to handle it. We women leaders can't afford a lack of emotional control to limit our leadership capacity.

HE'S NOT JUST ONE OF THE GIRLS

Oh boy, it was not one of my most stellar meetings. I had a dress on that day and felt all twisted up, literally. This was back in the day when it was common to wear pantyhose to work, and my particular pair was all in a twist and threatening to cut off the circulation to my right thigh. The meeting hadn't started yet and the room was full of women, so I scootched behind the table, hiked up my dress, and tried to straighten things out. Then the room got quiet. I looked up and realized Jim had just walked in. I had forgotten he was supposed to join us, and by the look on his face, he was wishing he didn't have to. I tried lamely to make a joke, which made everyone laugh, but it wasn't the wisest thing to do: it started the conversation rolling about the evilness of pantyhose and how surely they had been created by mean, sadistic men. It just went downhill from there as the conversation turned into something similar you might hear at a girls' night out.

Jim was a great guy with a great sense of humor. He was married and had grown up in a house full of sisters, so he laughed along with us, but he was unusually quiet for the rest of that meeting.

I learned something that day: the wonderful men on my team should not be expected to act like "one of the women," and I shouldn't treat them that way. Just as I sometimes feel left out or uncomfortable when a meeting seems as if I've wandered into the boys' club (girls not allowed!), I need to make sure I don't make any men on my team feel like outsiders among women.

As a leader, there are times when I direct not only the agenda but the climate and tone of the conversation. That day should have been one of those times. There are some men on your team who can roll with a girl conversation, but there are some who get as uncomfortable with topics women like to talk about as they do with an overload of emotion. As the leader, I need to be sensitive to that and do everything I can not to alienate them in their position on the team.

THE GUY-GIRL THING

We love how Sue Edwards, Kelley Mathews, and Henry J. Rogers cut right to the chase in their book, *Mixed Ministry*: "God did not create us male and female so we could tease or limit one another, but so that we could join together, two images of God combined to make a whole, and glorify him through our unity."[1] So why is this so hard? We want to find ways to work together, but many times the fear of doing something that might be interpreted as inappropriate or untoward makes us pause. Should I meet with him alone in my office? Is it okay for me to invite him to ride with me in my car to that meeting?

Sometimes we don't have to make these calls because our church or organizational policies will dictate our actions. But other times, the decision is ours. I'm not about to suggest that you put yourself in a situation that would make either of you or your spouse uncomfortable, but what I will suggest is that you don't let yourself fall into the trap of avoiding each other or limiting what you can accomplish together because you happen to be of the opposite sex.

I (Sherry) will be honest and say this is a subject I've struggled with and one that has stimulated a lot of discussion between my husband and me. I will always honor my husband in every work and social situation, but I also strive not to limit my leadership or the leadership of someone else on my team out of fear. I go back often to Edwards, Mathews, and Rogers, who urge Christian men and women who work together to remember that they are brothers and sisters because they come from the same family. Brothers and sisters in healthy relationships speak honestly and trust each other without a hint of sexual tension.

Have you found yourself avoiding the men on your team because it's uncomfortable or letting their sense of discomfort dictate your working relationship? Deal with it now. Have honest conversations. Involve your spouse, and make sure you are honoring him or her. Come to an agreement that doesn't limit your work together, within which you both can be comfortable and sure that you are honoring God. Are there rules in your church or organization that are limiting what you can accomplish together? Rules such as men and women not allowed to meet together in each other's offices or ride together to lunch meetings can be hard to work around, but they could be based on sound reasons or past events. Sometimes just talking them through can help both sides have a better understanding or even reach another solution. Have a humble, prayer-filled conversation with your pastor or supervisor where you speak honestly, with no hint of resentment or anger. State your position clearly and without heightened emotion. Be specific about how the current requirements limit your ability to move the organization's vision forward and listen with an open mind to the reasons for these rules. Don't go in insisting on getting your way. Instead, be humble, cover the situation with prayer, and continue to do your best.

ARE YOU LEADING OR BOSSING?

"Okay, let's move forward on this," I said. "Get your team going on the actions I just outlined. Let's start today." He paused, and then his answer caught me off-guard: "Are you asking me or telling me?" he asked with a smile. This guy was a strong team leader with brilliant ideas of his own, but I had just blown past his brilliance. I had assessed the situation quickly and in my confidence had seen the apparent solutions. But this isn't what he had come in for. He wanted to talk about the situation that was troubling him and share his thinking with me. What I had done was respond with an autocratic style that can send some people, men and women, over the edge.

No one, man or woman, likes to be bossed. But I've noticed men can be especially sensitive to this, especially when it's coming from a female leader. Without realizing it, I think we can come across as a nagging mom in our leadership style, forgetting that good leadership is not leading by authority or position, but by inspiration and empowerment. Men need to be respected, honored, and trusted, and simply telling them what to do isn't accomplishing this. When we come across as autocratic without respecting their wisdom, intelligence, and experience, we strip them of their dignity, which could generate their resentment and resistance.

Have you fallen into this in your leadership with men? Letting your position allow you to slip into an autocratic, nitpicking style that could easily be interpreted as bossiness? Sometimes the best thing we can do as a leader is to acknowledge, apologize, and reverse our course.

WHAT ABOUT THE BOYS' CLUB?

My (Jenni's) first introduction to the boys' club was early in my career in the music business. Opportunities for advancement and promotion were quite accessible in that environment, but there was still a social glass ceiling that indirectly hampered my ability to relate with the men I worked with: golf. When a contract needed to be negotiated, the guys would head to the golf course to work it out. When a major project was completed, the boys would golf to celebrate. All the while the other women and I were left back at the office trying to make sense of how they pulled one over on us again. Not to be outdone, my friend Kat and I decided we weren't going to be left behind any longer. It was time to learn how to play golf. We took lessons with great fervor. Our goal was to prove ourselves and eliminate every excuse to not be included.

To this day, I have not played a round of golf with my male coworkers. I'm almost tempted to feel defeated in sharing that with you, but let me tell you what I did learn: I learned that there are some things that I have the power to control and others that I don't. I had the power to learn to play the game of golf, but I couldn't control whether they would invite me to play.

The boys' club does exist in most organizations, but frankly so does the girls' club. We instinctively gravitate to those with whom we share the most interest, especially for social opportunities. So if we find ourselves outnumbered and feeling like an outcast, what should we do?

First, find a support sister. If you are struggling, it can be helpful to connect with another woman leader outside your work situation for prayer support and a reality check. Are you being too sensitive? Are you taking words and actions personally that are not intended that way? Sometimes talking it out with an objective sister can help you analyze and react with wisdom and maturity.

Second, resist the urge to pout, withdraw, or force your way in. Remember that no one controls your responses but you. If you are being excluded, don't respond with a tantrum or an overly emotional response, and don't force yourself into a situation that will make everyone uncomfortable. Do, however, accept the invitation if you are invited to join the guys, and don't assume they are just being polite. Relax, have fun, and be yourself with confidence.

WHAT DOES HE BELIEVE?

I (Sherry) listened with interest as a well-known pastor outlined why he didn't believe in women filling leadership positions in his church and had a rule that no women could be in leadership over any male past the age of twelve in his church. He wasn't being mean or hard-hearted and spoke with conviction, backing up his opinions with what he thought were justifying scriptural texts. I respect this pastor tremendously. I just don't happen to agree with him in this area and feel just as strongly that the Bible outlines a strong case for women leaders.

As I listened to this pastor, I was reminded that there are wonderful godly men in his congregation who share these same beliefs with their pastor. What if some of them come to work for me in the Christian organization that I now run? Will they struggle under my leadership because I'm a woman?

Perhaps you find yourself in a situation like this, working with a man who perhaps reports directly to you that has strong theological beliefs about women in leadership or feels you shouldn't be leading as a woman. If you lead in a church setting, we can assume your pastor affirms your leadership, but you may get negative feedback from other staff members, perhaps even other women. What should you do?

Take the High Road

Theological debates can be interesting but also exhausting and usually not productive. I love the way Jenni looks at this. She says that our goal as believers working together is to reflect the picture of beautiful biblical community, as Psalm 133 lifts up: "How good and pleasant it is when God's people live together in unity." This is what God designed us for, and it's critical for us to grasp this in relationship to our leadership and influence with men.

How true! I don't think it's our job to convince others of what God has called us to. I do think it's our job to face honestly our own questions and wrestle to the ground any uncertainties we may have about the leadership God has called us to. Exercising our giftedness as leaders is an important part of us as we help to create this biblical picture of community. If the men on your team have theological issues with your leadership, you can respect their views without moving aside in your leadership. Invite them to share their views with you and acknowledge them, but don't fall into the trap of false agreement or debate. Pray together, ask for wisdom, and then agree to disagree.

Don't Apologize

If God has called you to leadership, don't apologize for it. Be boldly humble. Acknowledge that not everyone is going to agree or affirm your leadership. Lead with the confidence that comes from knowing you have humbly submitted yourself to God and that he has your back.

THINGS WE NEED TO PAY ATTENTION TO

Certainly all leaders need to feel respected, honored, and trusted, and these affirmations are especially needed when it comes to leading men. With women, it's important to communicate that not only do you respect, honor, and trust them as a leader, but that you truly like them. With men, it's often in reverse order. I (Sherry) always try to communicate that I enjoy their friendship, but primarily I respect, honor, and trust their presence at the leadership table, always trying to communicate the ways they bring value to the team. I've noted that many women on my team are often looking for a level of friendship, and they receive value from our work relationship. The men on my team are often looking for fulfillment in the work itself. Here are some affirmations that a wise leader will pay attention to when working with men.

They Need Our Respect

I (Jenni) continue to learn the value of respect in my relationships, especially with leading men. Respect is most gained when it is frequently given. Currently I lead a team of four men, our executive team at Cross Point. Most of my formal leadership life has involved leading men rather than leading women. Probably one of the biggest lessons I've learned about developing a relationship of mutual respect with the guys I lead is that respect is earned, and it's earned over time. I can't expect every man I lead to instantly respect me. For many of the reasons that we've discussed in this chapter, both sides face hurdles in developing healthy relationships working across gender lines. Every time I enter into a new working relationship with a guy, I have to remind myself not to expect instant respect. I have to prove to that individual that I am worthy of his respect by first respecting him.

A couple of years ago, I was working with one of our leaders on a big project. It was a new situation for both of us, and I was admittedly a little extra high-strung and very attentive to all the details. I felt a tremendous weight of responsibility for the project and as a result asked numerous questions about details that I normally wouldn't be as involved in.

After a few weeks of my intensity, he came to me to express his frustration with the way he felt I was micromanaging the project. His concerns were fair, but so was the level of my involvement. I explained to him how my questions and attention to detail were not a question of his ability but part of my responsibility and accountability to our senior pastor and board of directors. That conversation did a number of things for our relationship:

- It reminded me that I needed to be more intentional to explain myself when I'm more involved in a project than normal. The unusual engagement from me led him to believe that I didn't trust him to do the job well. When I explained why I was more involved than usual, he fully respected my leadership.
- It gave him greater perspective for my role and responsibility, and as a result, he had much more respect for my leadership and the decisions I was making.
- It opened the door for more candid conversations in the future.

This leader and I now have more honest conversations about how we work together and as a result have much greater respect for how we each play our part on the team.

In this situation and others, I have learned that it's important for me to verbalize my respect to the men I lead. Many times I assume they know I respect them, but it's an unfair and naive assumption for me to believe they would know this information without my telling them. I've learned to verbalize respect to the men I lead by frequently identifying their strengths—both their personality strengths and their performance strengths. I make sure this affirmation is part of our biannual performance reviews, as well as part of my weekly meeting time with them.

Another important way to show respect to the men you lead is to include them on key information, perhaps even more information than they necessarily need for their role. When I take time to share the bigger picture behind a request or directive, they feel much more respected and are willing to engage it with more ownership. Many of the men I lead get bogged down by the details, but when I share the bigger purpose and the expected outcome of a project, they are much more willing to dive in fully. They can respect the process and their leader when they fully understand the purpose.

They Need to Feel Honored

We love the way God lays out what it looks like to honor another person in Romans 12:10: "Be devoted to one another in love. Honor one another above yourselves." I (Sherry) learned the power of this when I had the opportunity to lead a sharp young man who had been working in the organization for several years when I joined the team as his supervisor. He was energetic, enthusiastic, and hungry for more responsibility, and I knew I needed to invest some time learning about him.

I spent the first months observing and assessing. He was a gregarious leader who liked to process things aloud and felt honored that I took time to get to know him. I relied on several assessment tools to gain more information and requested the whole team share their results from the StrengthFinders Assessment as well as the DISC Profile.[2] Both tools helped me relate to his areas of strength and also the best way to communicate with him and the whole team. I learned he needed easy access to me throughout the day to bounce ideas off of, but also needed freedom to move forward on his own. He needed to know that I had made the effort to get to know him, so I coupled this with an early conversation, asking him, "How can I best support you and help you succeed?"

This conversation served both of us well. He knew I was on his side and appreciated that I took the time to learn and hear directly from him what he needed and what his particular work style was. I also made a concerted effort to honor his wife. I communicated what a privilege it was to work with her husband and that I would always be the biggest champion of their family. I encouraged her to feel free to come to me with any concerns she might have about our working relationship, and I asked her, "How can I best support and serve your family?" This conversation went a long way toward removing any sense of suspicion or mistrust and let her know something critical: I honored and respected not only her husband but their family. This has been one of the best working relationships I've ever had with a team member, and I'm so thankful that my actions were perceived as honoring.

They Need to See Our Trust

One of the ways my (Jenni's) staff at Cross Point has tried to put the importance of trust first within our culture is by creating an axiom, "Believe the best." The idea is that before we jump to conclusions about someone, we choose to first believe the best. We will assume the best about his or her character and intentions and then we'll immediately go to this person to clarify. Essentially we are starting from a positive point of view and saying, "I choose to trust you.'' We believe that choosing this perspective is an essential foundation for healthy relationships among our team.

The same is true with leading men on your team. When trust is given, trust is reciprocated. You can choose to trust rather than make assumptions based on misunderstanding, miscommunication, or misgivings. Take a minute to ask yourself these questions to see how you are doing in trusting the men on your team:

- Am I micromanaging any of the men on my team, giving the impression I don't trust them to make decisions on their own?
- Am I nagging or reminding too often, coming across as bossy or autocratic?
- Am I verbally conveying my trust to the men on my team and then backing it up with my actions?

If you answered the first two questions yes, today is the day to begin conveying a new level of trust to everyone on your team. Start by telling them why you trust them and their abilities, and then make sure your actions prove your words.

THIS CAN WORK!

The reality is men and women can work together in harmony in a way that honors God and his unique creation of male and female. But it takes work and a commitment to maturity and stellar leadership. Here are some closing encouragements.

Go the Extra Mile

The opportunity will always be yours as the leader to take the high road and extend courtesy and friendship even when it is not reciprocated. Just as a wife and mom sets the emotional tone of the home, it's your responsibility to set a healthy, godly tone in the work environment. Lead with respect, honor, and trust, making sure the men on your team not only hear these but experience them. In a misunderstanding, lead the way to reconciliation with good communication and honest conversation. If there is tension, take the initiative to find a resolution; be quick to listen and slow to anger. Let Hebrews 12:14 be your guide: "Strive for peace with everyone, and for the holiness without which no one will see the Lord."

Be a Grown-Up

There will be times when you'll have to take a deep breath and get over it. In any leadership situation, people will hurt your feelings. When you are leading a mixed-gender team, there is even more opportunity for misunderstanding and frustration. There will be times when you'll have to take your bumps and hurts to the Lord and choose to lean into the leadership maturity that comes from a secure relationship with God.

Grace, Grace, Grace

I (Sherry) was speaking at a conference where the conference administrator called all the presenters together before the conference began and said she was asking us to do three things: start with grace, give grace in the middle, and end with grace. She said she knew things were going to go wrong, and she was asking for us to expect it and be prepared with extra measures of grace. She was right (some of the conference details did go wrong), but she had prepared us well. Have you had this conversation with your team, both men and women? Let them know you know that both you and they will screw up. Sometimes you'll misunderstand each other, and other times you'll step on each other's toes. There will be moments when someone will be thoughtless and say something stupid. Ask them to live out Ephesians 4:32: "Be kind to one another, tenderhearted, forgiving one another, as God in Christ forgave you."

Stop the Blame Game

Here's the thing we women need to face: we have to quit seeing men as the enemy when it comes to our ability to lead. I (Jenni) know that some of you believe that the church, specifically the male leadership of the church, has historically held women back and inhibited their leadership. In many ways, you are right. Those things have happened. The degree to which that is true depends largely on your denominational background and experiences. But holding on to those historical events is only going to hold you back from leading well.

I believe with all my heart that God opens the doors to our leadership if we are faithful to his call and steward our part well. I have seen repeatedly in both my own life and the lives of other women leaders that doors open, resistance lessens, and opportunities increase when we are faithful to what God is asking of us right now, at this moment, for this season. If we can be patient, not get ahead of ourselves, or long for influence we don't have yet, we can be faithful to the opportunity for leadership in front of us. Every opportunity to lead, including every opportunity you have to lead men, is a critical step in bridging the great divide that exists between men and women. With every good experience we create, with every man who feels valued and respected through our leadership, we are diminishing that chasm between genders. Every good experience will replace a bad one. Every positive encounter creates a new perception. Everything you do will pave the way for the women leaders who will come after you.

QUESTIONS FOR REFLECTION AND DISCUSSION

1. What do you love most about leading or working with men? What's most frustrating?
2. Where do you need to grow most in working with men: controlling your emotions; overcoming bossiness; conveying respect, honor, or trust; or some other area?
3. Is there another area of tension in working with men that we didn't discuss in this chapter? What is it?

OVERCOMING THE COMMUNICATION BARRIER

Recently I (Jenni) was reviewing a stack of applications from women leaders who were going to be a part of a coaching group with me. One of the questions I asked was, "What topics would be most helpful for us to cover in our time together?" Do you know what the most common answer was? Communication. Their feedback suggested that we have a great many questions about our effectiveness and our confidence as communicators.

If you measured communication simply by how much we women talk, we should be great at communication. Some studies suggest that woman say three times as many words a day as men do. But we all know that communication is much more than talking, and that's where the challenge comes in. Communication takes on different forms, different interpretations, and different expectations by each person involved in it.

You've likely heard the phrase, "Everything rises and falls on leadership." If that is so, I submit that leadership rises or falls on communication. In everything we do, we communicate. Whether by words, actions, or attitude, we're constantly sharing messages with others. So it stands to reason that mastering communication is essential to our success as leaders. But communication can be complicated and messy. We are easily misunderstood and often misunderstand others. There are many nuances and subtleties to communicating well even in everyday relationships; couple that with the responsibilities of being a leader, especially a woman in leadership, and perhaps that is why my coaching group had this subject at the top of its list.

Merriam-Webster's *11th Collegiate Dictionary* defines communication as "a process by which information is exchanged between individuals through a common system of symbols, signs or behavior." Two things jump out in that definition. First, take note of that word *common*: it implies that the individuals exchanging information are speaking a shared language. If you've traveled to another country, you understand the importance of a common language. When I (Sherry) was in Barcelona, I wanted just a cup of coffee. Not cappuccino, not a latte, just coffee! I kept saying the word and they kept bringing me espresso, cappuccino, everything but plain old coffee. It made me want to scream. After a great deal of frustration and misunderstanding, I realized what I need to request was an Americano (their espresso watered down with hot water). Simple things, like a little caffeine fix, become complex when you can't effectively communicate.

The second thing to notice in our definition of *communication* is the next phrase "system of symbols, signs or behavior." Our common communication with others doesn't mean just language; it includes symbols, signs or behaviors, words, actions, and attitude. A study by the Caliper Corporation found that "the strong people skills possessed by women leaders enable them to read situations accurately and take in information from all sides."[1] Is it possible that our intuitive nature as women makes us more aware of the emotional dynamics surrounding communication? Could our sensitivity to how others feel or perceive our communication cause us to be that much more concerned with how we navigate communication?

Dawn Nicole Baldwin, founder and lead strategist for Aspire-One, a strategy and creative services firm, defines communication in this way:

> Communication is the channel in which vision is delivered. At its best it can serve as a rallying cry—informing team members which hill needs to be conquered, the role they need to play and why their efforts will make a difference. Truly effective communication defines boundaries, provides a clear target and a sense of what to expect. A stellar vision and strategy are only as good as they are understood. I've seen far too many teams lose momentum (or get derailed entirely) because of misunderstandings resulting in poorly cast vision. If you don't get your communication right, everything else will be an uphill battle.

In order to be effective as leaders, we have to speak a common language with our team—one that communicates vision clearly, serves as a rallying cry, defines boundaries, and sets expectations as Dawn suggests.

So where do we start in defining this common language? The heart of communication, we believe, is captured in two simple but weighty phrases: *to understand* and *to be understood*. This is really what communication is all about. Understanding is our common language with those we lead. When we can understand others—what they are saying and why they are saying it—we'll have a better chance of leading them well. In return, when we can be sure that what we're communicating is understood, we take tremendous steps forward in helping those we lead achieve our shared goals.

A great deal of complexity lies behind each of those statements, including the second point we identified from our communication definition. In our understanding of one another, we also have to understand how our nonverbal communication (our actions and attitude) is important. As we dig deeper into this simple phrase, *to understand and to be understood,* our hope is we'll unpack layers of communication effectiveness that will set you up to *just lead* even better.

TO UNDERSTAND AND TO BE UNDERSTOOD

Recently a friend and I (Jenni) were conversing over e-mail about an event that we needed to work on together. We swapped numerous details back and forth and then met for lunch to discuss it further. I was completely blindsided when my friend said that some of my correspondence in that e-mail had hurt her feelings. In sharing the details and specifics that would be necessary for the event, I had inadvertently conveyed a spirit of disinterest or unhelpfulness. My intention was to be thorough, but without any personal interaction in which she could hear my tone and read my nonverbal cues, she misinterpreted my message. I felt terrible!

It's human nature for us to expect others to understand our point of view. Our personal bias conditions us to expect that our view is obvious to everyone else. But you've been around the block long enough to know that that is anything but true.

One of the greatest gifts we can give to others is a willingness to seek to understand where they are coming from before we feel the need to be understood. Stephen Covey wisely taught us this in his book *The Seven Habits of Highly Effective People.*[2] Our influence with others is dramatically affected by this principle. It's the golden rule in action: "Do to others what you would want them to do to you" (Luke 6:3). Tim Elmore, founder and president of Growing Leaders, a nonprofit organization created to develop emerging leaders, explains it this way: "What most people really want is to be listened to, respected and understood. The moment people see that they are being understood, they become motivated to understand your point of view."[3]

This is exactly what happened when my friend and I sat down to talk over our communication misunderstanding. Once we heard where the other was coming from, we were both much more eager to understand one another's point of view. We clarified the points of misunderstanding and moved ahead with greater unity in our project.

As leaders, it's exceptionally critical that we do the extra work of seeking to understand others and then helping others understand us. There are a number of ways we can help bridge the understanding gap.

BE A GOOD LISTENER

"Listening may be the most important part of communication," shares Harriet Harral, a university communications center director, in the book *Five Leadership Essentials for Women*. She then says, "It is through listening that we validate each other. It is through listening that we create the opportunity to truly know each other."[4]

Listening is becoming a bit of a lost art. In an age where multitasking is exorbitantly praised and handheld devices buzz at us constantly, we've become used to conversations that are frequently interrupted or hijacked altogether by a seemingly more pressing need. Perhaps that's why finding a great listener is like discovering a rare gem. When you find such a gem, make that person your friend for life! I am privileged to have one of these kinds of friends. No matter the circumstance, how busy she is, or how many distractions are around us, the only thing that matters to her is what I'm sharing. Chances are you've encountered someone like this too. I've been tempted to think that individuals with this ability have a special gift that I don't possess, but I don't believe that's true. Good listening is a developed skill—something that every one of us can learn if we're willing to do the work.

Here are some simple things that you can do to listen to others more effectively:

- *Focus.* Turn off your ringer, or put your phone in your purse. Arrange where you are sitting so that others passing by do not distract you. Clear your mind, and devote yourself to the · other person.
- *Let the other person know you're listening.* Nod. Make eye contact. Rephrase or clarify important points.
- *Ask questions.* Your questions will affirm that you're listening while also ensuring that you understand correctly.
- *Observe the unspoken.* Is the other person nervous or anxious? Intense or timid? Stand-offish or leaning in? Her nonverbal communication will tell you a lot about how she feels about what she is sharing.
- *Keep an open mind.* Don't assume you know how the individual is thinking or feeling, don't jump to conclusions or judgments, and don't be quick to try to fix it.
- *Clarify what you heard.* Restate the key points the individual made. Then affirm them.

These tips for effective listening are applicable for nearly any type of conversation, but think of them specifically in the context of your leadership relationships. Do you give your staff the gift of your undivided attention? Are you quick to finish their thoughts or make snap decisions before they have shared all the details?

Our temptation as leaders is to hurry through conversations and make quick decisions; however, earning equity and credibility with your team is often best achieved through intentional listening. Resist the pressures that suggest you don't have time, and be more intentional with effective listening. Your staff will feel valued, and you may learn a great deal more in the process.

BE SELF-AWARE

In order to help others understand us, we must first understand ourselves. We've all encountered those heat-of-the-moment situations where we wish we could take back something we said out of frustration, hurt, or anger. Our emotions come out in a variety of ways. It could be the words we say, the tone or inflection by which we say them, or a nonverbal signal that we're not even conscious of. Dynamic leader Nancy Beach says it this way: "Most of us have blind spots about how we come across to others, and the huge challenge is to find ways to see ourselves more clearly and to identify where we are strong and where we need to improve."[5]

Several years ago for our annual staff retreat, we had a little fun presenting an award to everyone for something unique and fun about him or her. I (Jenni) received the "red neck" award. This is not the redneck that you're probably thinking of. I was raised in a small town in the Midwest, and I'm far from a good ole southern redneck. No, this red neck was in reference to the way my neck and throat turn bright red whenever something makes me anxious or frustrated. My team has discovered that they usually have fair warning of my level of frustration by the numerous shades of red my neck turns. I don't have to say anything. This nonverbal signal screams it for me!

Women are especially good at this form of communication. It's the look that your kids know means they are in big trouble when you get home. It's the cold shoulder you give your spouse when he disappoints you. It's when you shut down in a meeting because someone criticized or questioned your idea. Our nonverbal cues communicate a lot for us, often before we get the chance to verbalize what we're actually thinking.

That's why it's important to be aware of what you are communicating to others through your expressions, gestures, and body language. Is your face a dead giveaway that you dislike an idea?

Do you cross your arms when you don't agree with someone, put your hands on your hips when you want to convey strength, or roll your eyes when you're growing impatient or irritated?

Another part of nonverbal communication, especially for women, is our physical appearance. Fair or not, as a woman, our exterior gets scrutinized. An article entitled "How to Make a Great First Impression" said this: "While appearance for both men and women can be a key to their success, a survey by Women Work! found that seventy-five percent of the respondents believed that appearance at work affects how women are perceived by others more so than their male counterparts. Nearly eighty percent of the respondents also said that clothes, hairstyle and makeup can make a significant difference in their perceptions and confidence that a woman has the skills and knowledge to perform her job."[6]

Is what we're wearing distracting someone from hearing us? Do we convey professionalism, sex object, or sloppiness? With the constantly changing face of fashion, discerning this seems to be a moving target. Here are a few things that we do to try to hit the mark:

- *Wear clothes that fit.* Your wardrobe doesn't have to be extensive, but know what styles work well on you, and stick with those.
- *Don't go too trendy.* The workplace is not the best place to experiment with the latest fashion. Save those adventures for the weekend.
- *Accessorize tastefully.* Make sure your jewelry isn't louder than you are.
- *Keep things tidy.* Your dry cleaner, hair stylist, nail technician, and eyebrow waxer are your best friends. Keep regular appointments with them. You'll look your best and you'll feel more confident.
- *Consult your husband or someone else close to you.* As your greatest champion and fiercest protector, your husband is a great filter for discerning whether your appearance is appropriate. If you are not married, a mentor, friend, or parent may be a great person to consult.

- *Seek outside input.* Invite a trusted person you respect, who presents an image you'd like to emulate, to speak to the way you talk, dress, and come across. This can help you become aware of the things you're oblivious to.

The overall message that you want people to take away from an encounter with you is for your appearance to reinforce the things you do and say, not distract or overpower the real message you want to convey.

BE SENSITIVE

Perhaps one of the most complex parts of communication is in how we say something or emotionally respond to how someone says something to us. A *Harvard Business Review* article by Deborah Tannen, "The Power of Talk: Who Gets Heard and Why," shared this: "Communication isn't as simple as saying what you mean. How you say what you mean is crucial and differs from one person to the next, because using language is learned social behavior: How we talk and listen are deeply influenced by cultural experience."[7] Not only do we need to be sensitive to how we say things, but we also need to be sensitive to how others receive what we say.

Our sensitivity to how something is said can be triggered by circumstances that vary from person to person. We may hear something different than what the communicator intended because of built-in predispositions that are often based on our family dynamics and life experiences. Essentially we carry baggage into every act of communication. If you're insecure, you may read too much into what someone is sharing with you and feel threatened. If you had a parent who had difficulty conveying emotion, you might not feel comfortable sharing how you truly feel. If you once had a boss who was impossible to please, you may receive every directive from others as an overbearing impossibility. All of these reactions are baggage, and they prevent us from conveying and receiving messages effectively.

As leaders we have a responsibility to be sensitive to how our emotions are conveyed through tone and inflection. Although you might not actually say something unkind, your tone very well could have implied it. As Luke 6:45 says, "The good man brings good things out of the good stored up in his heart, and the evil man brings evil things out of the evil stored up in his heart. For out of the overflow of his heart his mouth speaks." I believe this scripture not only applies to the words we say but also the manner in which we say them. In his book *Enemies of the Heart*, Andy Stanley says, "Our hearts impact the intensity of our communication. Our hearts have the potential to exaggerate our sensitivities and insensitivities."[8] What is true in our hearts finds its way to the surface even if we are careful not to use actual words.

As leaders, our emotions come through in an unhealthy tone when we answer impatiently, react with visible frustration or anger, or respond condescendingly to someone who didn't meet our expectations. Can you think of a situation when you allowed your negative emotions to come through in how you spoke to those you lead?

But there is a good side to this as well. When the fruits of the spirit—love, joy, peace, patience, kindness, goodness, faithfulness, gentleness, and self-control (Galatians 5:22–23)—are an overflow of our heart, those things are also conveyed through tone and inflection. A person who exudes love and joy is contagious. You don't have to go around saying you love others or are joyful; it's clear in the way you talk and carry yourself.

As leaders, we have a clear choice in how we allow our tone and inflection to affect our communication with those we lead. When I'm tempted to respond with an unhealthy emotion such as anger or frustration, I've found that it helps to take a minute to collect myself and determine how I could respond in a more appropriate way. When I need to address an employee who didn't meet expectations, I can choose to share my disappointment with a spirit of gentleness and self-control rather than anger or impatience.

When you find yourself in a situation where your true feelings are oozing out through how you are saying things, find a way to take a break, process your feeling, and choose a fruit of the spirit through which to convey your message.

BE DIRECT AND CONFIDENT

Are you familiar with the age-old management tool called the "feedback sandwich"? It's a useful tool that suggests that if you need to deliver criticism to someone, it is best received if you layer it with two compliments: compliment, then criticism, then compliment. It's simple enough and usually quite effective. But as women, we have a tendency to make a different kind of feedback sandwich. Instead of a couple of slices of compliments and a little meaty criticism, we pack our sandwich with some big leafy romaine lettuce, a thick slice of tomato, cheese, peppers, onions, pickles, and spicy mustard. Before long, we've decorated it so much that the meat of our sandwich can no longer be found.

Dawn Baldwin describes this tendency as layering:

I think women need to feel more comfortable being direct. Many of us prefer to avoid potential confrontations, so our communications tend to be "layered":

1.   Ease into the conversation.
2.   Tend to the relationship.
3.   Communicate the point or purpose for the conversation (that is, the actual part that needs to be communicated).
4.   Ensure the relationship is still intact.
5.   Close.

Often I'm left trying to sift through these layers, wondering if she actually meant what she said or if she was trying to hint at something else.

Have you ever found yourself doing this: convoluting something you needed to say because you were afraid of how the other person would respond to it? I remember one time when I needed to have a tough conversation with an employee regarding his performance. I was dreading the conversation because the individual was rather sensitive and I didn't want to crush his spirit with the information that I needed to deliver. Unfortunately I couched the conversation with so much encouragement that he walked away without understanding that his job was in jeopardy. My layering resulted in a complete lack of clarity about the issue and led to conversations that were more painful.

Dawn goes on to share more thoughts on layering:

> In my experience, women have the tendency of not feeling comfortable saying specifically what they want. Instead, we tend to hint or provide vague generalities that are often misinterpreted. As George Bernard Shaw said, "One of the greatest problems of communication is the illusion that it has occurred." Communication breaks down for men and women when we don't say what we mean and mean what we say. My advice is to be as clear and direct as possible. Relationship building is important, but building a layer cake (or sandwich) with every conversation is not only unnecessary, it can slow down productivity. Your team will thank you.

Tannen's article provided strong support for the tendency we as women have to not be direct or confident in our communication. Tannen's research revealed that "women—like people who have grown up in a different culture—have often learned different styles of speaking than men, which can make them seem less competent and self-assured than they are." The idea here is that girls are raised to be more inclusive in relationships with other girls and will minimize their opinions in order to not make someone else feel less significant. Men are taught from an early age to jockey for position and influence. As a result, "Studies show that women are more likely to downplay their certainty and men are more likely to minimize their doubts."[9]

Watch for this tendency in yourself. When I'm anticipating a conversation in which I know that I'm going to be tempted to layer, I write out what I need to say ahead of time. I work to create concise and direct yet sensitive ways to share necessary information without overtalking. It's also helpful to rehearse it enough to feel comfortable with your language but not so much that you will repeat it from memory, which could cause it to come across as insincere. A few successful conversations will go a long way to boosting your confidence in lessening the layers.

PAY ATTENTION TO YOUR TIMING

As leaders, it's important for us to understand the significance of timing. A well-timed word of encouragement is absolutely life giving to your soul, and a poorly timed criticism can completely demotivate you or even derail you. Our words carry a great deal of power; when we choose to say them also has tremendous impact. The old adage that timing is everything couldn't be more true than in how we communicate with those we lead.

I (Jenni) wrestle with a tendency to be critical. I'm wired to see where improvements can be made, and I'm constantly pushing myself and my team to be better. There are elements of this that make me a great leader, but if I'm not careful, I can quickly frustrate and alienate my team. In an effort to help me slow down and keep my timing in check, I've adopted these two little phrases: *Be quick to praise. Be slow to criticize.*

In my constant striving for better and best, I can breeze over opportunities to praise my team for what is good. The right time for praise and encouragement is immediately after a job well done. Whenever possible, praise others for their work, and honor them publicly when you can.

As a leader in full-time ministry, Sunday mornings are an incubator for the importance of timing. One particular Sunday I found myself extraordinarily frustrated by numerous details that our team was missing. In an extreme moment of frustration, I unloaded my disappointment on one of our leaders who was responsible for managing the staff who weren't meeting expectations. A host of things was wrong with how I handled this, but the primary one was that this unfortunate individual took my verbal lashing and then had to go onstage to welcome the congregation to our morning service! Although he shook it off and handled himself with great professionalism, I learned a valuable lesson about the importance of timing and the impact it can have on those I lead.

In my experience, most leaders are either too critical or are not critical at all. Great leaders learn this balance. Criticism given in love and with good timing is extraordinarily valuable to those you lead. Well-timed critical feedback can be a tremendous growth opportunity and a huge trust builder. In fact, sometimes you have to resist the urge to critique everything and focus on the one or two most important issues that need attention. A wise leader also recognizes that your praise and encouragement mean more when those you lead know that you'll also step into the difficult conversations when necessary.

Since my Sunday morning faux pas, I've learned the value of Monday morning conversations. My team can trust that I will save more difficult conversations for a longer conversation in which we can discuss the situation in more detail. Many of these Monday morning conversations have become extraordinary relationship-building moments.

Being slow to criticize simply means stepping back enough to consider the best timing to share difficult information. Don't react in the moment or out of anger. Step back and choose the right timing to share your critique with love and kindness.

JUST BE YOU

When I (Jenni) worked in the corporate world I was often told, "Be tougher," "Fight harder," "Don't back down," and "Have stronger opinions." When I moved to ministry, I was told nearly the opposite: "Be softer," "Don't be so defensive," "Don't feel like you always have to win," and "Be more open-minded." There is merit to each statement and important things that I needed to hear in both of those lists, but ultimately all I heard was that I needed to try to be what everyone else expected me to be.

While we hope that you'll take away some great suggestions from this chapter about how to communicate better as a leader, the most important thing I hope you take away is to be you. Nothing you communicate as a leader will be effective if it feels inauthentic. An article said it this way, "Women cannot be afraid to address the issues that make them unique. We need women who are comfortable with leading from a place of authenticity."[10]

We realize that after a chapter full of suggestions on how to be a better communicator, finding your authentic voice can feel even more daunting. How do we keep all of these things—our words, actions, and attitudes—in mind as we try to understand and be understood? It begins to feel sterile, insincere, and formulaic doesn't it? Paula Nicolson made this recommendation, "Instead of fighting their natural instincts, women should embrace them because displaying emotional intelligence is the key to being a better leader."[11]

For whatever reason, God equipped us as women with a large dose of emotional intelligence and intuition. Trust your instincts, and don't shy away from them, especially when they may be different from those of your male counterparts. Look for clues about what is most consistent with your personality and style. What conversations do you walk away from feeling energized? Stop and think about what made those conversations life giving to you. Take a personality test and study your style. I've discovered that as an introvert, my best communication happens in one-on-one settings and when I've had time to think through the conversation in advance.

Discovering your authentic voice as a leader will be one of the most important steps in your leadership development. We can't lead well without sensitivity to how we communicate. Ultimately our goal as leaders is to communicate in such a way that we inspire and motivate others to do all that God has called them to. Great communication does just that!

QUESTIONS FOR REFLECTION AND DISCUSSION

1. What part of communication do you struggle with the most?
2. Where do you need to be more sensitive to how your emotions come through in your communication?
3. In what types of situations do others most commonly misunderstand you?
4. When do you feel the most comfortable or confident in your communication?

CHAPTER 10

PUT THE BOXING GLOVES DOWN

In a memory from my junior high days, I (Sherry) am walking as fast as I can down the corridor of Holman Junior School balancing my books, pencils, and lunch bag, with one thought pounding in my head: *Get to the lunchroom ahead of her.* It was a rivalry that had lasted all the way through elementary school, and I had never really figured out why Kim and I had never liked each other. We just didn't. As I landed breathlessly at the table full of seventh-grade girls, I heaved a sigh of relief. I had made it, and she hadn't. Good. And now there wouldn't be room for her at the table, and she wouldn't want to sit here now anyway because I was there. We were like oil and water.

Why was I being so competitive with this girl who had done nothing to me? It had started in kindergarten when she always got the answers right in our Blue Jay reading group (the big show-off). And it seemed to me the teachers always called on *her* more than they called on *me*. There was even an incident when I had stealthily dropped pencil shavings in her coiled braid on the top of her head in retaliation for getting to the toy box ahead of me, but that's a story for another time. Even as a young child, I couldn't put words to it, but I had an instinctive feeling that I needed to watch out for

Kim, that she was a threat to my very happiness. As I think back to these incidents in my early school years, I'm perplexed and more than a little ashamed. I'm not a mean person, but this little girl had gotten under my skin. Our relationship from the beginning was one of competition, both of us constantly vying to see who could get the best of the other one and gain the upper hand. I think back to Kim now and remember her as talented and smart and a nice person. What was my problem? Was it simply jealousy or something even bigger?

Fast-forward with me about twenty years as I stepped into one of my first leadership opportunities in women's ministry as a volunteer. We were planning a women's event and were in the middle of a planning session. As we talked about the goals for the day and the surrounding details, I shared a couple of ideas I had heard from another church that I thought would be great to try at our event. Some heads began to nod as other women agreed they liked the idea. Then someone said, "That sounds great, Sherry. How about if you lead that?" Without thinking, I replied, "I'd love to!"

As the meeting progressed, I could tell something had gone wrong. The leader of the meeting was shooting me dark looks, and a thick and heavy tension hung over the table. Had I overstepped my role as a volunteer by interjecting these ideas and agreeing to take responsibility for them? You bet I had. When the next planning meeting rolled around, I wasn't invited. I tried to strike up a conversation with the leader of the earlier meeting the next time we ran into each other, and I offered a sincere apology for overstepping her authority, but the relationship was never the same. I had challenged her leadership, and now I was *out*.

It may seem silly, but these types of incidents happen to women leaders every day, and they are hard to make sense of. In my own leadership, I've felt threatened by other women and also found myself on the other end where I was perceived as the threat. What's behind this? We know it doesn't make sense to worry that if we acknowledge another women as a great leader or even help her along the way, we are damaging our own leadership trajectory, but somehow there's a human instinct to feel threatened or challenged when another brilliant woman is spotted on the horizon. In many of us, it causes thoughts of, *What if they like her better than me? What if she takes over what I'm doing and I get kicked to the curb?* When thoughts like this come on the horizon, I picture Satan over in the corner rubbing his slimy hands together and laughing gleefully: "I've got her now!"

COULD THERE BE SCIENCE BEHIND THIS?

It's commonly recognized that competition exists between men, but how about between women? Women are often portrayed as nurturing, highly collaborative creatures who work and play well with others. But could there be more to the story? A recent study showed some disturbing behavior behind the sweet smiles and accommodating natures that many woman portray.[1] "I was convinced," researcher Tracy Vaillancourt said, "having lived my life as a woman, that we're not as pleasant as some people make us out to be."

In the study, forty women were gathered in a room and instructed that they would be involved in a discussion on female conflict. During the discussion, a conservatively dressed woman (the researchers named her Conservative Kari) walked in and called the research director from the room. In a separate room, another forty-six women were grouped together with the same instructions, but this time, "Kari" had a much more provocative dress and manner. The women's reactions were interesting but sadly predictable. The group visited by Conservative Kari showed no observable reaction at all. The group with Provocative Kari were observed gossiping, giving the woman a once-over, and engaging each other with negative comments or mocking Kari after she left the room. These reactions were witnessed in 97 percent of the participants in this second group.

In this study, the reason behind the behavior isn't totally clear. Perhaps the women saw Kari as a rival or just didn't agree with how she was dressed and it sparked a streak of mean behavior. Vaillancourt and Sharma suggest that women are intolerant of those who challenge their mind-set about acceptable behavior or appearance and use indirect aggression to shut them down.

WHAT'S BEHIND THIS MESS?

Blogger Haley Gray Scott suggests it may be due to a scarcity mind-set: "Anytime there is scarcity, there is a potential for derogatory attitudes that undermine the potential achievements of women, and nowhere is the principle of scarcity more at play than in Christian ministries and organizations."[2] Another study states, "Although women constitute over a majority of churchgoers (60 percent), men continue to dominate leadership roles in the church," with women making up only 15 percent of Protestant clergy.[3] So could a scarcity mind-set be leading to catfights among Christian women and leaders? Could it be that we feel an intense need to stand out in a minority and so take the small-minded path of making other women look bad in order to make ourselves look better? If you and I are one of only a few women in a leadership role at an organization, could we instinctively be led to attack each other in order to protect our place?

This scarcity thinking and the resulting feeling of competition could lead to a deficit in being able to connect with other women. In her book *Reinventing Womanhood*, author Carolyn Heilbrun suggests that the top reason women fail in achieving leadership positions is not due to a male-induced ceiling, but because women haven't learned to bond with each other. She states that women fail to support each other along the way and don't bring other women along through mentoring or through encouraging the organization to be more accepting of women leaders. Heilbrun says, "Women of achievement have become honorary men, having consented to be token women rather than women bonded with other women and supporting them."[4]

These are strong words and disturbing in a way that may strike some chords of truth. If you have been in leadership for any length of time, I bet you've witnessed or experienced this in some form or fashion. Maybe it's been a snarky comment from another woman about your appearance, your personality, or the way you lead that has come out of the blue and caught you off-guard. Perhaps it has been a sense of territorialism that speaks loudly: "This is MY area. Keep out!" Or perhaps you've even played a part, responding negatively to an instinctive "I need to watch out for her" kind of feeling.

THE THREE LEADERS YOU MAY HAVE ENCOUNTERED

The hardest part about attacks from other women is that you often don't see them coming. You are minding your own leadership business and then *wham!* you find yourself the butt of gossip, criticism, blatant defiance, or the cold shoulder. You are often left wondering, *What did I do?* and you begin retracing your steps to figure out what you could have or should have done differently. Sometimes the hurts and bumps of leadership can lead to these extreme reactions that perhaps you've seen in woman leaders or even yourself:

• *Shrinking Violet* withdraws her leadership out of hurt or fear. I have been in situations where I've bumped up against resistance or jealousy from another woman and thought to myself, *Well, I'll never do that again,* as in the case of my early experience as a volunteer. I found myself guarding what I said and my leadership so as not to draw attack from another woman who might not like it. I kept ideas or suggestions to myself because I didn't want to step on another woman's territory or kept quiet in a meeting because

I was afraid of what the reaction might be from other women at the table. Looking back now, I can see I was being a coward and not being true to who God called me to be. The truth is there will be times when people are not going to like me or agree with what I do. I can't control that, and it's not part of my job as a leader to do so. If God has called me to lead, I need to bring my best to the table every time with humbleness and a godly spirit letting God have my back.

• *Retaliating Rita* is fueled by a "how dare you!" attitude. This is particularly nasty because it perpetuates the problem. I've had hurt feelings from a run-in with another woman and felt myself being drawn to thoughts like, "I'm not going to let her get away with that!" and begin to spin plans of how to stop her cold. As you can expect, this only escalates the conflict. It's a dangerous road to go down, and yet so very human. It's natural to react in defense when you are attacked but God calls us over and over again to take the high road. I love how 1 Thessalonians 5:9–11 encourages us here: "God didn't set us up for an angry rejection but for salvation by our Master, Jesus Christ. He died for us, a death that triggered life. Whether we're awake with the living or asleep with the dead, we're alive with him! So speak encouraging words to one another. Build up hope so you'll all be together in this, no one left out, no one left behind. I know you're already doing this; just keep on doing it."

Don't you love how God thinks the best of us here, just as he also knows we're tempted to do the opposite and often do? The fact is that we have a choice at every intersection of conflict. When we encounter an attack from another woman, we can choose to react with the grace and love that can come only from a divine source, not our human heart. It can stop the vicious cycle.

• *Cynical Cindy* wraps herself in the hurt and rejection and lets it take root in her heart. She looks down the leadership road and sees nothing but resistance and conflict and thinks, *Why bother?* This one must break God's heart. God made women to lead and lead well. We are designed to be visionaries, encouragers, and champions of other women, even when it results in cost to our own leadership. I have found myself here as well, on the brink of a potentially volatile situation and wondering, *Is it really worth it?* Unfortunately, we'll never be able to completely avoid conflict, and it's never our ultimate goal as leaders to do so. The hurts are going to come, no doubt. But with God's help and the protection of hiding his word in our heart, it doesn't have to scar us or shut us down.

If you find yourself mirrored in one or more of these three types of women, as I have, take a moment to ask God to transform you through the renewing of your mind, as he suggests in Romans 12:2: "And be not conformed to this world: but be ye transformed by the renewing of your mind, that ye may prove what is that good, and acceptable, and perfect, will of God." Although we can't control the other Violets, Ritas, or Cindys out there, we can control ourselves and do our part to stop the vicious cycle.

Jenni's Story

The topic of women championing other women is one of the reasons Jenni and I decided to write this book. We were both tired of women who were great leaders but quick to participate in territorialism, jealousy, and nasty backbiting aimed at other women. As we were dreaming together about what this book could become, Jenni shared a story with me about how she learned the power of truly laying down the boxing gloves and becoming champions of other women leaders.

❖

How dare she! This young little whippersnapper of an intern had blatantly disregarded the chain of command and scheduled an event without my approval.

I (Jenni) was fuming from what I thought was a sense of responsibility to order and proper protocol, but I was fuming because I felt threatened and insecure. I quickly put this girl in her place with no question of how I really felt about her and went about my business with a satisfactory feeling: *I showed her!* A few months passed, and I overheard my boss talking about offering this girl a job at our company. I marched right into his office and boldly declared, "You cannot hire her!" Much to my dismay, he did and not only did he hire her, he put her in the cubicle right next to me!

For several weeks, I avoided her at all costs. I grimaced when I overheard her laughing and chatting with her clients on the phone and then, of all things, offering to pray for them (we worked for a Christian company)!

While I treated her with disdain, she showered me with kindness and generosity. I felt tormented by my conflicting emotions. I was clinging desperately to my grudge and perceived injustice while softening to her kind and Christ-like heart.

Honestly I can't remember exactly when we—or, more accurately, I—turned the corner, but somehow we did. Over the next several years, Kat and I developed one of the deepest friendships I've ever had. She is one of the most amazing leaders I know, and I'm a better leader because of her. We shared our leadership lessons together and learned from one another. Rather than an adversary, she became a trusted confidante on whom I now lean for wisdom and advice.

When I put my boxing gloves down, I found one of the kindest, truest, and sincerest friends I've ever had. Kat taught me the power of generosity and unity. She showed me that scarcity has no place and that there is more opportunity and more blessing from sharing our influence generously with others.

It's been over fifteen years since that girl Kat disrupted my world. I can't help but wonder how much differently my leadership life would look if I had not learned this lesson way back then. I certainly still find insecurity and scarcity creeping into my heart from time to time, but the blessing of that relationship is a constant reminder of the power of working together and championing each other. It's one of my most precious memories and life lessons.

A few years ago, this lesson came full circle for me. I observed some of the same tensions rising within one of the younger women I work with. As an extraordinarily gifted worship leader, she confided in me her feeling of jealousy and insecurity with the other women on our worship team. I shared my story with her and challenged her to find a way to invest in and generously support the giftedness of these other women. I challenged her to replace jealousy with generosity and see how God would use that in her life. I watched with such pride as she developed a monthly gathering for our women worship leaders. She vulnerably shared her fears and insecurities and challenged this group of women to be supporters and encouragers of one another rather than competitors. You can imagine the beautiful sense of unity that exists among that team!

I'm convinced that there is so much more that God can do through our leadership as women when we put the boxing gloves down and start championing one another!

CALL TO ACTION—MOVING TOWARD UNITY

In my head, I (Sherry) have a picture of a scene from one of my favorite childhood movies, *How the Grinch Stole Christmas*, when all the Whos in Whoville join hands and sing as a sign of solidarity after the Grinch stole every last Who-present and scrap of Who-ham. Wouldn't it be wonderful to call all the women of the world together to join hands at the same time and call a truce? I know this is way too naive, but instead of wringing our hands and doing nothing, we can start with ourselves.

We each have been entrusted with a circle of influence that includes our coworkers, friends, family, and community. Take this opportunity to ask yourself these questions:

- Do my female coworkers see me as their champion, whether they work for me or I work for them?
- On the teams that I'm a part of, whether as a volunteer or a staff member, do they know for certain that I'll put the needs and successes of the other women present before my own?
- Do my children and husband hear me affirming the accomplishments of other women?
- Do I encourage my church and any organizations I'm a part of to equip and champion other women leaders, even at the cost of my own leadership position?

In my own life, I've had to examine not only my actions but my motivations, and I've tried to implement the following practical steps.

Stop the Judging

A friend shared a story the other day of driving to a store and being frustrated at the lack of parking places. As she was cruising around the parking lot looking for an opening, a small sports car zipped past her and pulled into a spot clearly marked with a handicapped sign. My friend was outraged. How could this woman, who looked perfectly healthy, take up a spot intended for someone with a handicap? She saw no handicapped sticker anywhere on the car. She paused long enough to give the lady a disapproving look and with a self-righteous shake of her head, drove on to find a parking spot a few spaces down.

She was stopped short as she walked toward the store and passed the handicapped spot and noticed the woman struggling to get out of her car. My friend quickly saw the reason: the driver had no legs. And the handicapped sticker was there: my friend had just missed it! She was instantly ashamed as she realized she had judged this women in an instant of frustration without fully knowing the circumstances.

How many times as leaders have we judged another woman? We hear something or see something, and without checking the facts or even giving grace to the context or situation, we judge. It gets us into trouble many times and stings harshly when we're the recipient of it. What if we agreed together right now, as we read these lines as women who lead, to stop judgment and give grace—even when it's undeserved, just as God has extended to us so many times?

Look for Other Women to Champion

Do you constantly have your radar on for other talented leaders, even when it's a younger, sharper woman who may someday replace or outshine you? This is hard because it requires taking the reins of your ego and keeping your leadership aspirations under godly control.

I had this modeled beautifully for me by Betsy, a dear friend who served as a mentor to me in my early years of ministry. She was a brilliant speaker and writer but was always giving other women the chance to speak or write, putting them in opportunities where she could have done a brilliant job herself. I saw her time and time again speak words of encouragement that prompted another young woman to have the confidence to step into a leadership role without ever considering how this might limit her own opportunities.

Betsy had the ability to spot talent in others, even when they didn't see it in themselves. One time when we were preparing for a women's retreat, I asked Betsy to be the speaker for the closing segment of the retreat. She paused a minute and then quietly suggested the name of a woman who was new to our church. This was a curious choice to me: I didn't know this woman well, and I knew everyone would love to hear from Betsy. I also knew Betsy hadn't had the chance to speak in a while. But Betsy was adamant. "Let's give her a chance," she said. We did, and Betsy was right. This newcomer did a beautiful job, and it was a catalyst in her leadership growth. I picture Betsy in heaven someday surrounded by all the other women leaders she inspired and encouraged. And I think, *I want to be just like that.*

Affirm Other Women to Anyone Who Will Listen

I have another friend who reminds me of a lovely perfume— not because of her scent (although she always smells wonderful) but because of the feeling she leaves in the room after she's been there. In any conversation, she constantly uses words that affirm the accomplishments of other women. After spending five minutes with her, you're certain that she believes in women leaders and how they can change the world. And she's not choosy with whom she shares these compliments. She freely shares them with her friends, her coworkers, other pastors, and people she doesn't know. After she finishes a conversation, she leaves behind a fresh feeling of optimism that lightens the room.

Once I was standing in a group at a conference, and someone was complaining about the lack of women speakers and picking apart the few women who had been selected. My friend was quick to jump in with this comment: "But weren't they amazing? I love to hear great women speakers! And what a privilege to speak in front of such a big crowd. I think I'll go tell them right now what a great job they did!" And she did. After she left, the encouraging aroma of her conversation stayed with us for a long time, and I was reminded of the power of a few simple affirming words.

I want to be like that, known as a champion of women leaders without a hint of jealousy or pettiness. By believing steadfastly that women are great leaders and using my attitude, words, and actions to encourage and champion them, I'm doing my part to put down the boxing gloves. And I'm hoping you'll join me.

QUESTIONS FOR REFLECTION AND DISCUSSION

1. Have you had painful experiences with other women that have affected your leadership? How have you dealt with them? Have you brought them into the light?
2. When you face tension in leading other women, do you find yourself reacting as Shrinking Violet, Retaliating Rita, or Cynical Cindy? Is there another reaction that you deal with? What do you do about it?
3. When leading other women, do you struggle more with jealousy, judging, or being their champion? Is there another area that causes you difficulty? What is it?

CHAPTER 11

ENGAGING THE NEXT GENERATION OF LEADERS

At a recent meeting where about twenty young women ranging in age from twenty-one to twenty-eight had gathered, I (Sherry) watched one of the group members out of the corner of my eye and was quite fascinated by what I observed. The young lady had taken her shoes off, tucked one foot under her other leg, and was now popping her gum. Quite loudly. She wasn't bored or being disrespectful. On the contrary, she was being quite brilliant in her own relaxed way as she spoke in the discussion. Everyone there was a strong, brilliant woman with a passion for leading, but only two were leading in any capacity in their church. Why?

When I asked the question, they hesitated. I could tell they were gauging how much they should say. I again asked, "Why don't you lead in your church?"

The barefoot gum popper spoke up: "I don't always feel wanted."

I dug a little deeper: "Why wouldn't you be wanted? Churches are always looking for bright young leaders."

"Well, they say they are, but that's not what it feels like. My church said they wanted me to help on a leadership team, but

143

they didn't really have anything for me to do. I got bored, so I stopped."

Several heads nodded around the table, and others joined in.

"They ask for my ideas but then never do anything with them."

"It felt like they wanted me at the table just because I was young, but then they didn't know what to do with me."

"I didn't feel like they trusted me to really lead."

Unfortunately I'd heard all of this before. Young leaders were being invited by their church to lead but not given any influence or allowed to speak into the process. They sometimes ended up in areas that didn't connect with their passion or skills or match their capacity. Young women said they had come to the church with corporate or business experience, but were offered opportunities only to lead in women's or children's ministry, neither of which they felt called to do. Some said they felt held at arm's length by other leaders more because of their inexperience than even their gender. They were frustrated—frustrated because they knew they had good ideas and a level of insight that wasn't currently at the leadership table. But they weren't allowed to bring it.

WHY THE DISCONNECT?

One of the questions I get asked the most by churches is, "How can we find more leaders?" If churches are desperately seeking new leaders and young women are looking for places to lead, why aren't we connecting? Is it fear, lack of trust, or something else? John Ortberg suggests something else: "There is an old saying in the church world that the issue is never the issue; the issue is always control."[1] And when it comes to generations working together, the question of control is never more than about a micron below the surface. Ortberg goes on to say:

One researcher put it like this: we often think people are opposed to change, but that's not quite true. Everybody changes all the time—particularly when they are the ones proposing the change. It helps to distinguish between two types of change: technical change and social change. Technical change has to do with logistics and props. Switching from typewriters to computers, or pews to individual chairs, or hard copies to email are technical changes. Social change has to do with who is making the decision. Social change has to do with who is in control. Any time a technical change is made, it raises the issue of social change. Am I and my group gaining or losing our influence? Who gets to call the shots around here? If my influence is receding, then probably my sense of ownership and commitment will diminish as well.

So maybe when it comes to including the younger generation in key leadership decisions, there is a double whammy: a sense of fear and perceived loss of control on the part of older leaders, plus a lack of comfort with this different generation. And perhaps when it comes to young women leaders, there's an added level of discomfort. There may be theological questions about where women can lead and resulting gender tension that puts up more walls.

The next generation brings a fresh type of thinking that can broaden the existing horizons. But it can also crowd how we think leaders should think, look, and act. Adding younger women leaders to the picture can suddenly cause the older generation to pay more attention to the organization's dress code and meeting arrangements. Is it okay for a male leader to meet alone with a younger female coworker? Are we okay with more relaxed dress that reflects today's trends in new ways? These are tensions that the younger generation can bring into the work environment.

My mind goes back to my first week at MOPS International. I was walking around the office, attempting to match the forty-three faces with the correct names, and trying to impersonate someone who didn't look overwhelmed. I entered the Outreach Department, which specializes in engaging new churches and walking them through the initial process of starting a MOPS group. I had heard this team was young, articulate, and incredibly focused. I expected to find them engaged in serious conversations at the phones on their desks but instead saw something different. Where there would normally be chairs were balls. And not just any balls, but ginormous three-foot, blue bouncy things. And the young women sitting on them were talking and laughing; one was eating a cupcake made out of carrots and carob flour. I guess it was the surprise of the unexpected, but I was caught short. Really? This team sits on big blue balls instead of chairs? Well, they do, and they are one of my highest-performing teams. But my initial reaction was to assume they weren't working hard because their work style was different from mine. They celebrate often with food parties in their office, their loud laughter drifting throughout the entire office. They come to work in trendy outfits and are always on the cutting edge of the latest exercise and healthy eating trends. I now find myself attracted to their fun working style and wander down to their department whenever I need inspiration or an energy fix.

SOME IMPORTANT QUESTIONS

I think this pressure of generational differences in work, attitude, and communication style is one of the biggest issues we face in engaging leaders who will carry us into the future. They bring different thinking and a different way of processing and productivity, and at times they are going to poke at our conventions. They are going to show up for work all "tatted up" (this means covered in tattoos for those who mistakenly thought I was referring to a type of crocheting), with earrings in places that surprise us, popping their gum, and bouncing on balls. The question is not whether we need them there or whether they will bring critical value to the table; the question is, "Are we older leaders ready to get comfortable with being uncomfortable?"

Before you say a quick yes, think about the implications. If your answer is, *Of course I welcome a different way*, but then design an environment that demands they conform to *your way*, you may have another think coming, as my grandma used to say. My outreach ball-sitting team is brilliant. They get their work done, and then some. They have fun while they work. They are creative, ambitious, and passionate about what they do. What does it matter if they choose not to sit in chairs? And while we're at it, maybe the rest of us should try sitting a little differently. I have to admit that one day after everyone had left the office, I sidled into their department and tried out a ball. It really was big bouncy fun until I fell off and found myself on the floor. But I'm quite proud of myself for trying.

A meeting that happened just a few weeks ago involved another young woman on my staff. We were talking about ideas for an upcoming magazine issue, and in response to a suggestion, she quickly replied, "We've done that." Idea after idea came up, and to many of them, she responded, "That's old; we already did that!" It began to get a little irritating. But as I listened to her, I realized that what she was really saying was, *Let's think differently; let's go in a new direction.* She was right. We were stuck in a rut, and she was inviting us to come along a new path. I invited her to share her heart and gave her time to bring us into her thinking. I realized that what I had been doing until then was inviting her to come into mine, and after an invitation to really be candid, she let me know that my way of thinking wasn't really that attractive to her. Instead of getting frustrated when a young leader's actions, ideas, or thoughts aren't fitting our expectations, it might be time to ask another critical question: *As older leaders, are we ready to be challenged?*

Something similar happened when I took the time to listen to the young gum-popping member of the discussion group I described at the beginning of the chapter. When I asked why she felt as she did, she shared a story. Her church had expressed an interest in reaching out to millennials and had invited her and several of her friends to be on a task force to lead the charge. They met, did research, shared ideas, and came up with a plan. But then they weren't allowed to execute it. Why? I asked. She answered bluntly: "They didn't trust us." She went on to explain that the church required her to go through their leadership development classes and still didn't let her lead. She said she wondered if they were afraid to let her team move ahead on their plan because it was different from anything they had ever done before, though they hadn't said so. In fact, they hadn't said anything. Instead, they just kept putting them off.

In this case, there's no telling what the core of the problem was. Maybe the idea was crazy and needed more development. Maybe there was a lack of resources and the timing wasn't right. Or maybe this church had a low-risk tolerance and couldn't move ahead with a new idea that wasn't tested and tried. This leads to another critical question we have to ask ourselves as older leaders: *Are we ready to take a risk?*

In my work with church teams in Leadership Network's Innovation Lab, a large multisite church I worked with found a great way to allow its younger leaders to try new ideas in an environment that didn't put the whole organization at risk. It put the younger leaders in charge of smaller worship venues that were large enough to yield results but didn't have an impact on the whole congregation until they had been proven. In these venues, they tried new worship styles and new ideas in programming and stage design. The strategy was brilliant. The younger leaders were allowed freedom to lead, and the older leaders were there to guide and give feedback. Risk was encouraged because the impact was mitigated, and if an idea didn't work, they all took the time to learn from it.

SO WHERE CAN WE START?

If you've tackled these issues with confidence, you might be wondering, *But where can we find these younger leaders, and how do we engage them?* John Ortberg says, "We can never move to where we want to be without speaking honestly about where we are."[2] The place to start is with current reality.

Assess your existing leadership structure. Do you have a good representation of young thinking, both male and female? Are there younger women present who have significant leadership responsibility? Do they have a respected voice at the leadership table? I recently talked with a pastor who suggested they didn't need younger women leaders at the executive level because the younger male pastors who were at the table all had wives and could voice their wives' opinions. Another pastor said they weren't worried about having younger leaders at the executive level because they often surveyed their younger generation, so they were confident they knew how they felt. These are poor substitutes, if they can count as substitutes at all. If you don't have young men and women involved in your organization's leadership and you're looking for them, here are some things to think about.

Place Your Trust in People, Not Experience

I recently heard a fascinating talk by Angela Ahrendts, chief executive officer at Burberry, the iconic London luxury clothier that is one of the one hundred largest companies in the United Kingdom.[3] When she stepped into the position in 2006, the company had grown stale. She felt it had lost its competitive edge and needed a younger image. She moved a younger, less experienced executive to the front lines as her chief technology officer and commissioned him to "help us think young." He launched a social media strategy that gained Burberry an unprecedented presence on Facebook, putting its clothing line in front of its target audience, and generating conversation that catalyzed its growth. This wasn't the only move Ahrendts made to think young. She engineered a "trading-seats" approach that moved younger staff to key decision-making roles and commissioned her older, more experienced team members to "guide but follow."

It was a bold move because these young leaders didn't have proven experience to lean on, but Ahrendts said it demonstrated the values of Burberry: *instinct, intuition,* and *trust.* She said in the early days that she learned to invest her trust in her people, not their experience, and to listen, especially to younger voices. She said she learned to ask critical questions and then to really listen to the instinct embedded in the answer. If a leader, regardless of age or experience, brought laser-sharp instinct and on-target intuition to the table, Ahrendts would trust them. She ended her talk with this wisdom: "The biggest mistake a leader can make is not listening."

When looking to engage the next generation of leaders, are you willing to trust in them even though they can't always prove their trustworthiness up front? If you demand complicated hoops of classes, training, lengthy shadowing, or apprenticeships before they are given the reins, they may just shrug their shoulders and walk away.

Pay Attention to How You Speak

Angela Ahrendts says, "The older generation speaks business, the younger generation speaks social."[4] She noticed when she took over Burberry that the company had been founded on proven business principles that drove everything from financial to marketing models. While this was sound, it didn't connect with the younger generation of leaders, who related everything in business to the social movements on Facebook, YouTube, and Twitter.

Ahrendts continues to encourage other companies not to be intimidated by how fast the world is changing, but to let younger leaders bring you along. She says, "You don't have to find your way to the cutting edge. Let your younger leaders lead you there." This takes a willingness to learn and the ability to trust. She said she depended on her chief technology officer to know the social media world and let him lead with his instincts. This resulted in an in-house marketing video spotlighting a popular British band that was edgy and different from anything else Burberry had ever done.[5] It went viral in a matter of days, and soon everyone in Britain was talking about Burberry. If Ahrendts had stuck with the conventional, she would have urged the team to pass this through marketing tests beforehand. She would have leaned into the proven business practices she knew before allowing the launch. But she didn't.

Ahrendts acknowledges that one of the biggest challenges can be not forgetting your heritage: "It sometimes seems that you need to scrap everything you've learned and everywhere you've been to take on a younger image, but this isn't wise."[6] She encourages companies to build on who and what they are as they bring young leaders aboard, making sure they have time to be steeped in the heritage of the company but still encouraged to think outside any parameters this might imply. In doing this successfully, she describes Burberry as "a young, old company."

Use Your Shoulders

I once had the privilege of interviewing Nancy Ortberg, Menlo Park pastor and leadership development consultant, and will never forget asking her this question: "What's the single most important thing you can do to encourage younger leaders?" Her answer was brilliant: "Help the younger generation lead by allowing them to stand on the shoulders of your experience so they can see farther than you ever could. Ask them what they see and allow it to shape your current reality."

I've thought about this often. I have experience, and younger leaders have new ideas. I have wisdom, and younger leaders have a relevance borne from living on the edge of what's next. I have knowledge of the tried and true, and they have a drive to innovate where no one has gone before. How can we bring these things together to benefit not only ourselves but the organizations we lead? Here are some things I'm trying.

Never Lead Alone

This one is hard for me because I often don't pause in my leadership; I just lead. I've been trying to remind myself to slow down, invite a younger leader to accompany me to a meeting or on a trip that is outside their responsibilities—not so that they can watch me but so that I can gain from their input. I like to ask, "What do you see that I don't? What would you do in this situation? What are your thoughts on this?" When I've taken the time to do this, their insight has blown me away.

I remember a conversation I had with a young team member I had invited to travel with me to a conference I was speaking at. On the long flight home, we talked about the conference and my session. I asked for her opinion, and she candidly asked some great questions. Why had I chosen the topic I had spoken on? Why hadn't I been bolder in my presentation to talk about the sensitive issues related to the topic? She listed three or four areas that she wished I had addressed, all of them bold and thought provoking. Her observations were spot on, and I found myself wishing I had consulted her before I had given my talk. I shared what I knew about the audience and the churches represented, which was great learning for her because she had not grown up in church and had not gone to church conferences in the past.

There's no doubt that two heads working together are far superior to just mine alone, but it also is encouraging for young leaders to step into opportunities they wouldn't get any other way. They get practical lessons that go beyond their own experience, which builds their confidence, competence, and capacity.

Encourage, Encourage, Encourage

This one comes more easily for me because I've had wonderful people encourage me, and I have experienced the power of it. Especially for young women leaders, catching them doing something good and then acknowledging it or bragging about them to the rest of the team is powerful. Speaking favorably about their leadership in such a way elevates their confidence and ability, especially when it's tied to a specific action or decision. I love it when, in response to a young leader's hesitant, "I don't think I can do that," I reply, "Why not? I think you'll do fabulously!" and I see them stand just a little taller. If you are an older leader, let your shoulders serve you well. Use them to elevate and encourage.

Operate in Reverse

One of the big lessons from my roundtable discussion with the young women leaders was that they didn't feel their opinions, views, or expertise were really valued. A book I've found invaluable is *Reverse Mentoring* by Earl Creps.[7] He encourages older leaders to align themselves with a younger one, not to mentor but to be mentored. He cautions older leaders to not try to be cool and hip but just be real. Some of his tips include these:

- Go ahead and admit you're not young, because you can bet the younger generation is already well aware of it.
- Ask questions, and give value to the answers they offer.
- Become a humble student, opening your mind to what you don't know you don't know.

This has been hard for me. I've had the privilege of being in mentor relationships with younger leaders at their request, and I love any opportunity to speak to their leadership. But flipping this relationship, where I invite them to freely speak to me, can be itchy. It's not that I don't know I need it, but I'm wired to return their input with feedback of my own. It's hard not to slip back into the role of the mentor. I have to remind myself to listen, truly listen, and then apply. Period.

The benefit of this to younger leaders is that they can tangibly see that their thoughts and opinions matter; this is especially so to young woman leaders, who often feel as if their input is overlooked and undervalued. One of my favorite things to do is to circle back around and give specific feedback on how their thoughts and suggestions helped me. I recently sent an e-mail to a young woman who had spent time with me and shared her thoughts, telling her how much she had shaped my thinking on a particular decision. Her reaction was surprise, and she responded, "Wow, I didn't know you trusted me that much!" I do, and it's a great reminder to me to always let them know.

ENCOURAGING YOUNG WOMEN

As we've mentioned often in this book, women make great leaders. They have the talent, intelligence, ability, and wisdom to not only lead teams, but step into executive leadership of organizations and congregations. Over the past years, I've paid attention to organizations and churches that have a preponderance of not only young leaders but use women in high levels of leadership. What do they do differently? How do they equip, encourage, and open the doors for these women to step up?

Dave's Story

One of the churches that has inspired me is Community Christian in Naperville, Illinois, where lead pastor Dave Ferguson has long been a champion of leading sharp, gifted women to their full capacity. Community Christian was one of the first churches to name a young woman as pastor over a multisite campus, with full leadership and teaching responsibilities. It was a bold move, and in his story, Dave shares how he has continued to look for other women with strong leadership abilities and calling.

❖

"No one has ever asked me that before," Jayla said to me with a look of shock. I had just finished teaching a workshop with Alan Hirsch based on our book, *On the Verge*.[8] As soon as we finished, Alan commented to me about one of the participants, "She is very sharp; you should talk to her about planting a church through NewThing." I agreed. He was referring to an African American woman in her late twenties who was sitting toward the front and had asked several insightful questions.

After the workshop, I introduced myself to Jayla and struck up a conversation. I learned how she became a Christ follower; how God consistently put her in places of influence and her passionate desire to trade her life for the mission of Jesus. I was impressed. So as we were walking out of the building, I asked her the question I have asked hundreds of other young leaders: "Have you ever thought about planting a church?" She literally stopped walking. Her eyes opened wide. She shook her head and replied, "No one has ever asked me that before." Jayla went on to explain that in the churches she was a part of, this was not a possibility: women didn't lead and didn't plant churches.

My conversation with Jayla has been burned into my conscience as a reminder of something that is very wrong! I know if there was a sharp young twenty-something male with obvious leadership potential orbiting in the circles I travel in, he would have been asked dozens of times if he had ever considered planting a church. But not her!

Rather than explore why she had not been encouraged to lead, I want to focus on two reasons that it's important that, starting today, we encourage young leaders like Jayla to maximize their leadership potential.

First, Ephesians 2:10 reminds us that "we are God's handiwork, created in Christ Jesus to do good works, which God prepared in advance for us to do." God's Word assures us that every single one of us has an important reason for being on this planet. When God birthed us, he birthed us with a purpose for our life. There is something very important that God meant for each of us to do—a "good work" that will contribute to the accomplishment of his mission. But if we continue to encourage only men to excel in leadership and exclude women like` Jayla, we will be standing in the way of the good work that God wants them to accomplish. The truth is that many of us who are in church leadership have stood in the way of hundreds and thousands of women doing the "good works, which God prepared in advance" for them to do.

Second, Jesus's last challenge when he left earth was for his followers to "go into all the world" (Matthew 28:19) and accomplish his mission. I'm more convinced than ever before that if we are going to accomplish this mission, it will require every gifted leader we have, both men and women. As a pastor and someone who understands the full weight and responsibility of "rightly dividing the word of truth" (2 Timothy 2:15), I'm convinced that leadership is not something reserved for men. And from a practical perspective, it's like the church is trying to accomplish its mission with one hand tied behind its back.

Why are we trying to do this with only half our available leadership? It's stupid! We need to maximize every leadership resource we have for the mission of Jesus.

It was four years ago that Tammy Melchien began sensing that God was calling her to plant a campus of Community in Chicago. Up to that point, we had not been successful in planting campuses in the city, and all of our locations were in the suburbs. We knew we needed just the right leader to launch this important new site. Tammy, like Jayla, was a bright young woman whom God had continually put into positions of influence. But unlike Jayla, Tammy had received encouragement to lead and had done so in ministries inside and outside the local church. Like many of our other staff, Tammy raised her own salary to join our team and proved that she could start something from nothing. In every role we gave her, she not only excelled personally, but did an outstanding job of developing other leaders around her.

Over the next nine months, she began talking to my brother, Jon, and me, who lead Community, about the call she felt to start this campus in the heart of the city. We agreed that Tammy was the right leader to start a new campus in the Lincoln Square neighborhood. Jon, who would oversee Tammy, also saw this an opportunity to influence other church leaders to give women leaders executive leadership opportunities.

Tammy has done an outstanding job launching this new site, building relationships with the local school and neighbors, teaching and preaching on weekends, and continuing to develop leaders around her. Our dream is to one day see two hundred locations of Community in the city and suburbs of Chicago, and I believe God used Tammy to give that dream a real possibility by establishing our first site in the city. It was Tammy's initiation that ultimately resulted in Jon's relocating his entire family to the city and starting a network of three Community sites in two years. Being a catalyst for a movement and the campus pastor of Community-Lincoln Square is the "good work God prepared in advance" for her to do. Without Tammy in that role, the mission would be hindered and our church held back.

As Dave's story illustrates, it makes a profound difference when the executive leader and staff encourage young women to step into all that God has called them to be as leaders. If you're a pastor or executive leader reading this book, we'll assume you already believe women can lead and would like to affirm and encourage the women leaders in your organization. Let the words of this book encourage you to use your shoulders of experience to affirm and elevate the women around you. Be a champion of women leaders, even in the midst of some Christian cultures that would have you think and do otherwise. Do all that you can to seek out sharp young women, encouraging them to boldly step into their gifts and offering growth opportunities that will help them hone their gifts. Encourage your experienced leaders to share their knowledge freely and make space for the next generation to lead.

But what if you're a gifted woman leader who knows you're called to lead but haven't been given the opportunity? Perhaps it's been painful to read these words, knowing you are a leader but in an environment where it's not encouraged or allowed. What should you do?

Invest in honest evaluation. If you find yourself in a situation where your leadership is completely and repeatedly blocked, there may be times when it is necessary to seek another organization or church within which to lead. But be careful here. You don't want to find yourself running from place to place with a persecuted chip on your shoulder. If a change needs to be made, cover it with careful prayer and self-examination beforehand. Ask yourself some candid questions:

- Is my gender or age really an issue, or do I need to do some work on my attitude?
- Have I done everything I can to develop myself as a leader, and do I always bring my best to the table, or have I succumbed to a victim mind-set?
- Is God leading me to another opportunity, or is he calling me to stay put and help change the culture?

These are not easy questions. I encourage you to seek a trusted mentor or wise friend to help you with honest objectivity in your evaluation. These questions can prove to be valuable to your leadership development when you give them honest evaluation.

Don't give up! Wherever God puts you, ask him for wisdom and a humble spirit to approach your leaders with the offer to help in whatever capacity they will use you. Then bring your best game to the table with faithfulness and a willing attitude. As we've mentioned throughout this book, the best defense is an awesome offense. Be the best leader you can be, even if your leadership opportunity is small. Don't whine, don't get defensive, and don't pout. *Just lead.* Seize every opportunity to grow in your leadership. Continue to encourage the women around you, and be their champion. Don't fall victim to a scarcity mind-set, instead lead with excellence and courage, knowing God is enough. He's called you; he'll make a way.

CONCLUSION

We hope you've been inspired by this book. Leadership is a high calling and privilege, and we hope our words have encouraged and stimulated your thinking. Jenni and I are your biggest cheerleaders, and we're praying for you. Don't give up. *Just lead!*

QUESTIONS FOR REFLECTION AND DISCUSSION

1. Do you have young women leaders in your church or organization? If you don't, why do you think this is so? If you do, what's worked for you that you could offer to others?
2. What do you think holds most young women back in their leadership?
3. Do you personally encourage young women in their leadership? Why or why not?

NOTES

Chapter One: Only the Lonely

1. Mike Bonem and Roger Patterson, *Leading from the Second Chair* (San Francisco: Jossey-Bass, 2005).

Chapter Two: I'm Not Afraid

1. Veggie Tales, "God Is Bigger Than the Boogie Man," http://www .metrolyrics.com/god-is-bigger-lyrics-veggie-tales.html.

Chapter Three: The Monster You Are Avoiding

1. "Jessica's Daily Affirmation," YouTube, 2010, http://www.youtube .com/watch?v=qR3rK0kZFkg.

Chapter Four: You're Not Doing It Right

1. ThinkExist.com, Quotations Online, 2012, http://en.thinkexist .com/quotes/theodore_roosevelt/.

2. Brene Brown, *The Gifts of Imperfection* (Center City, MN: Hazelden, 2010), 39.

3. Bianca Juarez, "In the Name of LOVE" blog, December 22, 2009.

Chapter Five: Growing Pains

1. George W. Bush, *Decision Points* (New York: Crown, 2011).

2. John C. Maxwell, *The 21 Most Powerful Minutes in a Leader's Day* (Nashville, TN: Thomas Nelson, 2000).

3. Mark Batterson, *Wild Goose Chase: Reclaim the Adventure of Pursuing God* (Colorado Springs: Multnomah Books, 2008), 50.

Chapter Six: Make Up Your Mind Already!

1. ThinkExist.com Quotations. "Napoleon Bonaparte quotes." Think Exist.com Quotations Online, October 1, 2011; November 26, 2012, http://en.thinkexist.com/quotes/napoleon_bonaparte/2.html.

2. John Tierney, "Do You Suffer from Decision Fatigue?" New York Times, August 21, 2011, http://www.nytimes.com/2011/08/21/magazine/do-you-suffer-from-decision-fatigue.html?r=2.

3. For this quote from Terry Gulick, see http://www.braindash.com/quotes/terri_gulick/if_its_meant_to_be_its_up_to_me/.

4. Christine Caine, "Taking The Leap of Faith," blog, October 13, 2011, www.equipandempower.org.

Chapter Seven: Go Big or Go Home

1. Winston Churchill, *The Unrelenting Struggle* (London: Cassell, 1942), 274–276.

Chapter Eight: Leading Men

1. Sue Edwards, Kelley Mathews, and Henry J. Rogers, *Mixed Ministry: Working Together as Brothers and Sisters in an Oversexed Society* (Grand Rapids, MI: Kregel, 2008).

2. StrengthFinders Assessment: http://www.strengthsfinder.com. DISC Personality Profile: http://discprofile.com

Chapter Nine: Overcoming the Communication Barrier

1. "The Qualities That Distinguish Women Leaders" (Princeton, NJ: Caliper Corporation,, 2005).

2. Stephen R. Covey, *The Seven Habits of Highly Effective People* (New York: Free Press, 1989).

3. T. Elmore, *Habitudes for Communicators.* (Atlanta, GA: Poet Gardeners Publishers, 2012).

4. Harriet Harral, "Communication Essentials," in Linda Clark, comp., *Five Leadership Essentials for Women* (Birmingham, AL: New Hope Publishers, 2004), 37.

5. Nancy Beach, *Gifted to Lead* (Grand Rapids, MI: Zondervan, 2008), 110.

6. Nina Jamal and Judith Lindenberger, "How to Make a Great First Impression," *business know-how*, n.d., http://www.businessknowhow.com/growth/dress-impression.htm.

7. Deborah Tannen, "The Power of Talk: Who Gets Heard and Why," *Harvard Business Review*, September–October 1995, 138.

8. Andy Stanley, *Enemies of the Heart* (Colorado Springs, CO: Multnomah Books, 2006 and 2011).

9. Tannen, *The Power of Talk*, 139, 142.

10. Cheryl Isaac, "The Next-Generation of Female Leaders Will Emerge at a Faster Pace When Women Stop Trying to 'Act Like Men,'" *Forbeswomen*, January 27, 2012, http://www.forbes.com/sites/worldviews/2012/01/27/the-next-generation-of-female-leaders-will-emerge-at-a-faster-pace-when-women-stop-trying-to-act-like-men/.

11. Quoted in ibid.

Chapter Ten: Put the Boxing Gloves Down

1. Tracy Vaillancourt and A. Sharma, "Intolerance of Sexy Peers: Intrasexual Competition Among Woman," *Aggressive Behavior* 37 (2011): 569–577.

2. Haley Gray Scott, "Christian Catfights: Why Christian Leaders Don't Support Each Other," *Hermeneutics*, January 2012, http://blog.christianitytoday.com/women/2012/01/christian_catfights_why_women.html.

3. Blogger Haley Gray Scott quoted from the White House Project Report, 2011, on the blog "Patheos" on February 6, 2012: http://www.patheos.com/blogs/jesuscreed/2012/02/06/womens-view-of-women/.

4. Carolyn G. Heilbrun, *Reinventing Womanhood* (New York: Norton, 1993).

Chapter Eleven: Engaging the Next Generation of Leaders

1. John Ortberg, "The Gap," *Leadership Journal* (Summer 2009). http://www.christianitytoday.com/le/2009/summer/thegap.html?start=1.

2. Ibid.

3. Angela Ahrendts, "Choices," Chic Fil A Leadercast simulcast, 2013.

4. Ibid.

5. "London Streets: Burberry Autumn/Winter Campaign 2012," video, http://www.youtube.com/user/Burberry.

6. Ibid.

7. Earl Creps, *Reverse Mentoring: How Young Leaders Can Transform the Church and Why We Should Let Them* (San Francisco: Jossey-Bass, 2008).

8. Alan Hirsch and Dave Ferguson, *On the Verge* (Grand Rapids, MI: Zondervan, 2011).

RESOURCES

Books on Leadership

Beach, Nancy. *Gifted to Lead: The Art of Leading as a Woman in the Church.* Grand Rapids, MI: Zondervan, 2008.

Edwards, Sue, Kelley Matthews, and Henry J. Rogers. *Mixed Ministry: Working Together as Brothers and Sisters in an Oversexed Society.* Grand Rapids, MI: Kregel Publications, 2008.

Saxton, Jo. *More Than Enchanting.* Downers Grove, IL: InterVarsity Press, 2012.

Scazzero, Peter. *Emotionally Healthy Spirituality.* Nashville, TN: Thomas Nelson, 2006.

Books on the Theology of Women in Leadership in the Church

Bilezikian, Gilbert. *Beyond Sex Roles.* 3rd ed. Grand Rapids, MI: Baker Academic, 2006.

James, Carolyn Custis. *Half the Church: Recapturing God's Global Vision for Women.* Grand Rapids, MI: Zondervan, 2010.

ABOUT THE AUTHORS

Jenni Catron serves as the executive director of Cross Point Church in Nashville, Tennessee, a ten-year-old multisite church. She leads the staff of Cross Point and oversees the ministry of its five campuses. Previously she worked as an artist development director in the Christian music industry for nine years.

Jenni's passion is to lead well and inspire, equip, and encourage others to do the same. She is the founder of Cultivate Her, a community whose purpose is to "connect, engage and inspire" women leaders. She speaks at conferences and churches nationwide, seeking to help others develop their leadership gifts and lead confidently in the different spheres of influence God has granted them. Jenni blogs at www.jennicatron.tv and contributes to a number of other online publications as well.

She loves a fabulous cup of tea, great books, learning the game of tennis, and hanging out with her husband and their border collie.

❖

Sherry Surratt is CEO and president of Mothers of Preschoolers International (MOPS), an organization that equips and encourages young women as mothers and leaders. Prior to joining MOPS, she served as director of innovation at Leadership Network, a Dallas-based organization that helps church teams implement new ideas in ministry. She has an extensive background in education and ministry and served for eight years on the staff of Seacoast Church, a multisite church in Mt. Pleasant, South Carolina.

Sherry is passionate about women reaching their potential in mothering and leadership and maximizing their potential in their families, their communities, and the world. She speaks at conferences and churches nationwide and is a contributing author to *MomSense Magazine*, a publication for young moms, and also blogs at sherrysurratt.com.

Sherry knows that coffee is the ultimate beverage and loves hanging out with her pastor husband, her two children and daughter-in-love, and her granddaughter, Maggie Claire.

INDEX